THE MINIATURE SCHNAUZER

Phyllis DeGioia

Project Team
Editor: Lexiann Grant
Copy Editor: Joann Woy
Design: Stephanie Krautheim
Series Design: Stephanie Krautheim and Mada Design
Series Originator: Dominique De Vito

T.F.H. Publications
President/CEO: Glen S. Axelrod
Executive Vice President: Mark E. Johnson
Publisher: Christopher T. Reggio
Production Manager: Kathy Bontz

T.F.H. Publications, Inc.
One TFH Plaza
Third and Union Avenues
Neptune City, NJ 07753

Printed and bound in China

06 07 08 09 10 1 3 5 7 9 8 6 4 2

Library of Congress Cataloging-in-Publication Data
DeGioia, Phyllis. The miniature schnauzer / Phyllis DeGioia.
p. cm.
Includes index.
ISBN 0-7938-3645-X (alk. paper)
1. Miniature schnauzer. I. Title.
SF429.M58D44 2006

  636.755--dc22   2006017811

This book has been published with the intent to provide accurate and authoritative information in regard to the subject matter within. While every precaution has been taken in preparation of this book, the author and publisher expressly disclaim responsibility for any errors, omissions, or adverse effects arising from the use or application of the information contained herein. The techniques and suggestions are used at the reader's discretion and are not to be considered a substitute for veterinary care. If you suspect a medical problem consult your veterinarian.

The Leader In Responsible Animal Care For Over 50 Years!™
www.tfh.com

TABLE OF CONTENTS

HISTORY
of the Miniature Schnauzer

Schnauzers have consistently been a popular breed over the past 600 years. These energetic terriers who love to lounge in people's laps started out as German farm dogs. They excelled as ratters in particular, but no vermin in the vicinity were safe when the Miniature Schnauzer went to ground.

On German farms, the larger Schnauzers helped out by pulling carts and guarding livestock, but they also hunted pests. However, the smaller Minis were better ratters and offered general vermin-ridding assistance. In a day and age without sufficient sanitation, the capability of a dog to eradicate vermin was critical. Most farms needed an indoor ratter, and unlike their larger incarnations, the Miniatures fit better inside the smaller homes of the era. Thus, the Miniature Schnauzers began their ascent (or descent in the opinion of some farmers) to family pets.

DOWNSIZING
The miniature variety began when fanciers of the Standard

Schnauzer bred smaller Standards with Affenpinschers (known as *Diablotin Moustachu,* or mustached little devils) and small, fluffy, black Poodles. Some historians of the breed believe that the little wolf Spitz, the Miniature Pinscher, and the Wire Fox Terrier all got their paws into the action. Frankly, no one is exactly sure what breeds were used to downsize the Schnauzer to Miniature, but we know it's not just a case of pairing of smaller dogs.

Just before the turn of the 20th century, the Miniature Schnauzer was first exhibited as a breed differentiated from the Standard Schnauzer. The Giant Schnauzer also sprang from the Standard Schnauzer, but of the three sizes, the Miniature is the most popular.

Viewed as a companion dog, some people are surprised at the Miniature Schnauzer's desire to chase small moving critters; some are unpleasantly surprised when they find little corpses strewn about, although the industrious terrier views them as love gifts to be acknowledged by his owner. Vermin eradication is hardwired, so it's best to adjust and get used to it, because you will never be able to train the hunting instincts out of your Miniature Schnauzer. Let the dogs be the exterminators they were meant to be.

Even now, after the breed's evolution to a companion dog, he needs regular exercise, as appropriate to his active origins. He can certainly outrun people on those little legs, who manage only to dodder along behind this speeding bullet. After a bout of exercise, he will then indulge in a long snooze in some comfortable place like your lap or your neck, if your armpit is not available, which is perhaps why some people call them mini schnoozes. The couch will do nicely, too.

Popularity by the Numbers

The Miniature Schnauzer is not only well known and easily identifiable to the general public, but the registration numbers prove the breed's enduring popularity. In the United States, England, and Germany, the Miniature Schnauzer is currently ranked as one of the 20 most popular breeds.

GERMAN HISTORY

In Germany, the Miniature Schnauzer is known as *Zwergschnauzer* (*Zwerg* means dwarf). The Schnauzer is recognizable in artwork from the 15th century—even Rembrandt used a Schnauzer in one of his works in the 1600s. Germans saw how effective British terriers were at getting rid of vermin and at being good family companions. As a result, Germans wanted to create the perfect farm dog: an intelligent working dog who liked to please people, and who had a rough coat for protection from the elements. Schnauzers of all sizes have always been considered working dogs in Germany.

In 1879, a dog named Schnauzer won the Wire-Haired Pinscher

class at an international dog show in Germany, and the breed was eventually named after this particular dog's call name. In 1895, the first breed club was formed in Cologne. Called The Pinscher Klub, it defined the Pinscher to include both wire-haired and smooth-haired dogs.

Showing remarkable freedom from specifics, puppies from one litter could be registered as Miniature Schnauzers, Miniature Pinschers, or Affenpinschers, depending on their physical appearance. By 1898, a Pinscher-Schnauzer Klub emerged, which continues to this day. This club has as members the owners of all three varieties of schnauzers (miniature, standard, and giant), German Pinschers, Miniature Pinschers, and Affenpinschers. Their stud book showed that Jocco Fulda Liliput, probably a tiny little thing in their view, was the first Miniature Schnauzer registered. About a year later, the Miniature Schnauzer breed was formally shown for the first time, just in time to debut at the end of the century.

Dramatic, efficient, and companionable, the Schnauzer has found his way into every aspect of people's lives for centuries, from ridding farms of vermin to posing for paintings to warming laps.

World War I halted breeding efforts for most dogs in Europe, as did World War II, both of which nearly resulted in the end of some breeds. After World War I, interest in the little Schnauzers rose again. An interesting change that has occurred since the early days of the breed is that the first Miniature Schnauzers had a variety of coat colors that are no longer seen in Schnauzers of any size. These colors included reds, black and tans, yellows, and partis, all of which are mentioned in the records. Today, the breed standard calls for a coat color of salt and pepper, black and silver, or solid black.

Basic Statistics

Weight: 11 to 20 pounds (5.0 to 9.1 kg)

Height: 12 to 14 inches (30.5 to 35.6 cm)

Appearance: Sturdy and robust

Colors: Salt and pepper (most common), solid black, black and silver

Coat texture: Wiry with a soft undercoat

Tails: Docked

Ears: Uncropped in Great Britain; show dogs cropped in United States, pets optional

Grooming: Significant

Barking: Can be significant

Intelligence: High

Energy level: Fairly high

Exercise needs: Daily

Dog aggression: Not in well-bred dogs

With people: Very attached

With children: Good (best if the children arrive first), but always supervise young children

Popularity: Consistently high over centuries

Skills: Earth dog trials, agility, obedience

Congenital health concerns: Cataracts, microphthalmia, entropion, progressive retinal atrophy (PRA), Comedones syndrome, megaesophagus, muscular dystrophy, persistent müllerian duct, von Willebrand's disease, and factor VII deficiency

Life expectancy: 12 to 14 years

Country of origin: Germany

AMERICAN HISTORY

In 1920, the first Miniature Schnauzer crossed the big pond to the United States, only to die soon after his arrival. A gentleman named W.D. Goff, of Concord, Massachusetts then imported some Miniature Schnauzers in 1923, the era of Prohibition and speakeasies.

The next year, a bitch named von Cyriaksburg and her two daughters, Lotte and Lady v.d. Goldbachhöhe, immigrated to the United States. These beautiful dogs became the foundation of the breed in America. The first litter born in America whelped in 1925 and was sired by Mack v.d. Goldbachhöhe out of Amsel v.d. Cyriaksburg. The litter was born at the famed Marienhof Kennels.

In 1925, an era of good times and booming economic growth, fanciers created the Wire-haired Pinscher Club of America (WPCA), which included both Standard and Miniature Schnauzers. The year 1926 was an active year for the breed in the United States. The WPCA retooled itself to become the Schnauzer Club of America. Miniature Schnauzers were placed in the same class with the Standards for a little while, and both were shown in the Working Group. That fall, the Miniature Schnauzer became a separate breed, with its own breed standard. The Miniature Schnauzer was placed in the Terrier Group, while the Standard and Giant Schnauzers remained in the Working Group.

BRITISH HISTORY

In Britain, the Miniature Schnauzer's advent was just a few years behind the breed's move to America, arriving in England in

In the UK, the Miniature Schnauzer was first recognized as distinct from the larger Schnauzers in the mid 1930s.

All over the world, Miniature Schnauzers are beloved as smart, affectionate, non-shedding companions who also make classy show dogs.

the late 1920s. A black bitch named Enstone Gerti van Duinslut was imported by a gentleman named Mr. Hancock.

The Miniature was first recognized in the United Kingdom as independent from the bigger Schnauzers in 1935, during the American depression and pre-war concerns in Britain. The breed has remained a favorite in Britain and is shown in the Utility Group of the Kennel Club.

In 1935, during the early years of the breed in Britain, the formal name of the breed was changed to *Affenschnauzer*. This was done because Affenpinchers were used in the breeding down of the size of Standard Schnauzers. The name change did not sit well with fanciers, however, and only lasted for a year until it was changed back to Miniature Schnauzer. A rose by any other name apparently did not suit the Affenschnauzer.

REGISTRIES

The American Kennel Club (AKC), the United Kennel Club (UK), and Britain's Kennel Club are not country clubs for rich dogs, but instead serve a purpose as a registry. Registries make the purebred dog world go round. Mixed breed dogs cannot be registered. Puppies of registered dogs mated with other registered dogs can be registered as purebreds. If a puppy's mother and father are not registered purebreds with papers, the puppy cannot be registered with one of these recognized groups.

The AKC is the biggest registry in the United States, followed by the UKC. The registry also puts on dog shows, provides public education, and sponsors legislative efforts. Participation in sanctioned show events, such as conformation (where dogs are compared to and judged against their breed's standard), require that participating dogs be registered. Additionally, a registry publishes official standards for each breed, so that breeders know the genetic goals toward which they strive.

All a registry does is prove a lineage from registered parents; it does not indicate anything else. A registered puppy is not necessarily a high-quality dog or a healthy one, just as a registered puppy is not necessarily a low-quality dog or a sick one. Being registered does not affect health, temperament, intelligence, or other related factors. It simply means that the dogs in your particular puppy's the family tree are registered and their heritage can be traced.

If you want to participate in conformation dog shows, you must have a registered dog. If you don't want a show dog, or prefer such competitive activities as agility and obedience to conformation shows, the registration is pretty much worth the paper it's printed on in terms of what it means to the dog's life. Unregistered purebreds and mixed-breed dogs can participate in nonconformation events with groups other than the AKC.

A very important aspect about choosing a purebred dog is in ensuring predictability about the breed's traits. If you want an active, smart, funny, affectionate, nonshedding rat-killing lap dog who requires a lot of grooming, that is what you'll normally get if you select a Miniature Schnauzer. They are not bred to retrieve or point or herd or race. Although some of them can do those things, those characteristics aren't standard for the breed. Burrowing after little critters and digging holes in the process is predictable for a Miniature Schnauzer, as is an affectionate, intelligent, feisty nature.

The American Kennel Club (AKC)

Created in 1884, the American Kennel Club (AKC) classifies Miniature Schnauzers in the Terrier Group. The American

Ear Cropping

To crop or not to crop—this is a hotly debated question.

The Kennel Club does not allow cropped ears in the show ring unless the dog was born outside of the United Kingdom and imported. The Miniature Schnauzer standard of the Kennel Club calls for ears that are "neat, V-shaped, set high, and dropping forward to the temple." The AKC standard says "When cropped, the ears are identical in shape and length, with pointed tips." The UKC standard states "Ears are set high on the skull and may be natural or cropped," which means that cropping is optional. The surgery is strictly cosmetic and not medically necessary. Some people have come to believe that ear cropping should not be done, while others believe it enhances the dog's appearance sufficiently for the surgery to be worthwhile. (By the way, it's normally the breeder's responsibility to crop ears, not the buyer's.) Uncropped ears are rarely, if ever, seen in the show ring in the United States because of a popular preference for the cropped look. Some breeders, like Pat and Jim Discher of PJ's DogHouse in Darlington, Wisconsin, crop show dogs, but not pet-quality pups.

Breeder Karen Brittan of Britmor Miniature Schnauzers in Oak Grove, Minnesota, says "I used to feel that all Schnauzers should be cropped and that the breeder was out to make a buck if he didn't crop. After more than 30 years of having ears done, I have grown to love a pretty uncropped ear, hate the aftercare of cropping and what was done to the dog, and now do not crop at all. Talk about a turnaround!"

Miniature Schnauzer Club (AMSC), a member club of the AKC, was formed in 1933. The AKC is based in New York City. Its objective is to promote the sport of purebred dogs The club sanctions events in which participants can enjoy competitions with their canines. The members of the AKC are dog breed clubs—parent clubs—not individual persons.

A parent club is a group of fanciers dedicated to a specific breed. These people are interested in promoting better knowledge and understanding of the qualities of their chosen breed; parent clubs licensed by the AKC meet requirements that allow them to offer AKC events and titles. The AMSC is the national parent club for Miniature Schnauzers.

The United Kennel Club (UKC)

In 1898, the year Teddy Roosevelt and his Rough Riders charged up San Juan Hill, the United Kennel Club (UKC) was formed with the idea of a total dog in mind, meaning a dog "that looks and performs equally well." Miniature Schnauzers were accepted into the Terrier Group of this body in 1948. Performance programs include such events as conformation, obedience, agility, field trials, water races, hunting tests, and more. The UKC is a bit more informal than the AKC, and the UKC pushes for owners to handle their own dogs during events rather than use professional handlers. The UKC promotes itself as being user-friendly. The club is based in Kalamazoo, Michigan.

The Kennel Club

Begun in 1873, in Queen Victoria's London a few years after the death of Charles Dickens, the Kennel Club is the main registry for the United Kingdom. The Kennel Club classifies the Miniature Schnauzer in the Utility Group, which indicates a fitness for a specific purpose, such as ratting. The breeds in Utility have been bred to perform specific functions that are not included in the Sporting or Working classifications. The Kennel Club educates the general public and dog fanciers about responsible dog ownership and puts forth legislative effort for canine health and welfare.

Fédération Cynologique Internationale (FCI)

While many people have only heard of the American Kennel Club, Kennel Club, and perhaps some other national kennel clubs,

These Mini Schnauzers have uncropped ears.

A Moustached Snout by any Other Name

Why was the name *Schnauzer* chosen for this breed? Several potential reasons come to mind. One definition of Schnauzer translates from German into English as "walrus moustache." Before laughing too hard at this translation, compare a walrus's face or a Civil War-era drooping moustache to a Schnauzer's face. The tusks and moustache are remarkably similar in style to the Schnauzer.

Another reason is that the German word *Schnauze* can mean muzzle or snout in English. Historically, English *snout* and German *Schnauze* have the same linguistic origin; the German word means the *snout* of an animal, and "muzzle" is used specifically when referring to the snout on dogs.

According to Dr. Bernd Guenter, a dog fancier who lives in Germany and writes dog books in the English language, a man's moustache is a schnauzbart—schnauze/snout + bart/beard—or in the short colloquial form, schnauzer, because the moustache grows on the snout. Schnauzer facial hair can be short, like old-time movie heartthrob Errol Flynn's, or walrus-like, resembling Otto von Bismarck's, the founder of the German empire.

The Schnauzer breed gets its name from its moustache, or snout-beard. "The image that comes to my mind most immediately when thinking of *schnauze* is a pig's nose," said Guenter. "There is an old German verb *schnäuzen* that means 'blow one's nose,' and an old German word for handkerchief is *schnauztuch.*"

Germans take their mustaches so seriously that they regularly hold competitions, such as the World Beard and Moustache Championships, so it is no surprise that they would name one of their most popular breeds after its most prominent facial feature.

an international organization actually exists. The Fédération Cynologique Internationale is the World Canine Organization, which includes 80 members and contract partners (one member per country), each of which issues its own pedigrees and trains its own judges. The founding nations were Germany, Austria, Belgium, France, and the Netherlands. It was first formed in 1911 but disappeared during World War I. The organization was reconstituted in 1921. Currently, neither the United States nor Canada is a member.

The FCI ensures that its pedigrees and judges are recognized by all FCI members. Every member country conducts international shows as well as working trials; results are sent to the FCI office, where they are input into computers. When a dog has earned a certain number of awards, he can receive the title of International Beauty or Working Champion. These titles are confirmed by the FCI. The FCI recognizes 331 dog breeds, and each of them is the "property" of a specific country, ideally the one in which the breed developed. Each breed's owner country writes its breed standard, in cooperation with the Standards and Scientific Commissions of the FCI; the translation and updating are carried out by the FCI. In addition, via national canine organizations and the FCI, every breeder can ask for international protection for his or her kennel name.

THE MINI SCHNAUZER TODAY

Despite his origins in one country, the Miniature Schnauzer is bred throughout the world. Not every breed can claim so many fanciers or such universal appeal.

While the breed is still quite capable of ratting and doing general farm work, he is more likely to be seen as a companion and family dog. His primary job is no longer the eradication of vermin, although he will certainly do that, given the opportunity. He excels as an alert watch dog but is always ready to play and have fun.

He prefers being with his people to being with other dogs. You can't go anywhere in the house without him, and he will not let you contemplate the contents of your refrigerator without his company. It is also likely that he will accompany you even into the bathroom. Unlike some terriers, he is vocal but not aggressive and usually plays well with other dogs. A Schnauzer's appeal is in his intelligence, affection, sense of humor, outgoing disposition, size, and sheer personality, which is much larger than the dog himself.

The ears of these Miniature Schnauzers have been cropped so that they remain upright and pointed.

CHARACTERISTICS
of the Miniature Schnauzer

The Miniature Schnauzer physically resembles the Standard and Giant Schnauzers. Put all three beside each other in a lineup, and it would almost look like trick mirrors were being used. Minis are about a foot (0.3 m) tall at the shoulders, so they are little guys—the word "miniature" is certainly appropriate—but don't think for a minute that you won't notice them much because they're little.

Despite his smaller stature, the Miniature Schnauzer appears robust—healthy, full of vim and vigor, and ready to leap into action from a nap at the sound of a fly buzzing by. They have the voice power of the larger Schnauzers, which can be a good thing or a bad thing, depending on your point of view and whether or not you're taking a nap.

TOO CUTE

Miniature Schnauzers are really cute! It's the facial hair, of course, that makes their appearance so distinctive. Those huge walrus mustaches and beards are just beautiful, and the bushy eyebrows add a lot of dash. The Miniature Schnauzer has an expressive face, and emotions easily play across it.

When awake, they look like they've just enjoyed an espresso and will have another one as soon as their busy schedule allows it; when they're asleep, they look like angels. However, these guys are pistols and will make you laugh every day, even if you're having a bad one.

Their vibrant, feisty personality is incredibly endearing. Oh, and did I mention that they're cute?

PHYSICAL DESCRIPTION

Mini Schnauzers are adorable, and they know it. Their faces are inquisitive and expressive, and your first glimpse gives you an impression of energy, robust health, and an endearing demeanor. Their moustache and beard combination, while not unusual in the dog world, is accented enough here for the breed to be immediately recognized. Mini Schnauzers are the definition of cute!

The Shape and Size of Things

A robust, sturdy terrier, the Miniature Schnauzer is about 12 inches (30.5 cm) high and weighs between 13 to 20 pounds (5.9 to 9.1 kg). In proportion, his body is somewhat square.

The head has a bit of a rectangular shape, accented by wonderful whiskers. A full walrus-type moustache and a beard complement the overall look. The brown eyes are oval in shape and very expressive, particularly when you have food in your hand.

The Miniature Schnauzer is a sturdy though small dog who is big on personality.

Ears and Tail

The AKC standard allows for either cropped or uncropped ears, but it does call for a docked tail. Ears may flop over at the tips, be an upside down V-shape when uncropped, or stand erect if cropped. The tail is docked to be short, but those 2 inches (5.1 cm) or so that are left are long enough to be expressive— and these guys are very expressive!

Historically, the tail of the Miniature Schnauzer was docked to keep it from being injured in the field. Cropped, upright ears were meant to be attractive rather than having any utilitarian purpose. Today, it's a personal decision whether or not to dock tails and crop ears.

Many Americans are moving toward a preference for uncropped ears. This trend

What Is a Breed Standard?

A standard describes the perfect example of what a dog of a particular breed is supposed to look like. The Miniature Schnauzer standard paints a written portrait of exactly how a perfectly bred Miniature Schnauzer should appear.

If you are planning to show your dog, conforming to this standard matters a great deal; that's why showing dogs is called a conformation trial. If you are not competing in conformation or breeding, matching the standard doesn't make a difference (except in matters of health and temperament). Miniature Schnauzers who do not match the standard are referred to as pet quality, and these are perfectly wonderful dogs who can provide a lifetime of devoted companionship.

The standard for each breed describes in detailed language what each part of the dog's body should look like. Nothing is left to the imagination—ears, tails, coat, eye shape, weight, height, and so on are covered in detail. Standards usually cover a dog's outline, head type, temperament, and movement. Herding or working breed standards cover function, but because today's Miniature Schnauzer is bred to be a companion dog, function is not addressed.

Characteristics that disqualify a dog from the conformation ring are listed, such as being too tall or short, or a color that is not recognized.

seems to apply mostly to pet dogs, because most American Miniature Schnauzers in the conformation show ring have cropped ears. However, many people now feel that docking and cropping are not only unnecessary but painfully inappropriate.

The Kennel Club does not register any dog with cropped ears unless the dog was born and cropped outside Great Britain, and the procedure was done before the dog was registered with the KC. Even when dogs with cropped ears are registered, they are not permitted to compete in any Kennel Club activity.

Although many breeders in the United Kingdom still have it done, not all British Miniature Schnauzers have their tails docked. It is illegal for breeders to dock the tails of Kennel Club-registered puppies themselves—the docking must be done by a veterinarian.

In the United States, experienced breeders sometimes dock their puppies' tails for themselves so that they can decide precisely where the tail should be trimmed for the best appearance and closest conformation to the AKC standard. Other breeders have their veterinarian do the docking, yet may be present during the procedure to indicate where they wish the tail to be docked.

The size of the puppy determines how much of the tail is removed, because the tails of show dogs must be of a length that is appropriate to the dog's overall size. Undocked tails should stand up a bit and curl over the back.

Docking is typically done at 3 or 4 days of age. Ears are usually

Miniature Schnauzers are groomed for the show ring to dramatize certain features, like eyebrows, beard, and on this dog, cropped ears.

cropped when a puppy is 8 weeks old. The procedure can be painful, especially for sensitive dogs. The American Animal Hospital Association (AAHA) is against either procedure when done for strictly cosmetic reasons and encourages the elimination of docking and cropping from breed standards.

Coat Cut and Color

Miniature Schnauzers have a double coat. The exterior fur is wiry, and the undercoat is softer. The coat is trimmed short on the body, but the longer hair on ears, legs, and edge of the body—the *furnishings*—are retained. According to the AKC, UKC, and Kennel Club, the only acceptable colors are salt and pepper, which is the most common, solid black, and black and silver, which is uncommon.

Miniature Schnauzers can be found in other colors such as white, tan, rust, phantom, parti, chocolate, speckled, and multi-coats. There is nothing wrong with these dogs, but they are not Miniature Schnauzers as recognized by legitimate registries.

A white Miniature Schnauzer can be registered with the AKC as "other color" if both parents are registered, but the American Miniature Schnauzer Club, the parent club for the breed, does not recognize this color. If you plan to compete with your dog in AKC, UKC, or Kennel Club shows, understand that white and other color variations are not accepted, so choose a puppy with a coat sanctioned by the breed standard.

Just as West Highland White Terriers are defined by their white color, Schnauzers shown in conformation are defined by a given range of colors that does not include any variation from the typical silver or black combinations. However, if you have no intention of showing, these dogs make fine companions and performance event participants. The white color may become recognized some day, because fanciers of white Schnauzers are currently campaigning for recognition of these dogs. Standards and regulations are not set in stone and changes do occur, although the process can take a long time. So think carefully about what you want to do with your dog before you choose a color or possibly risk imposing limitations on what events you can enter.

Amount of Shedding

Miniature Schnauzers are often described as non-shedding dogs. Although that's not entirely true, they don't shed very much—just a tiny bit—and it is generally unnoticeable. Compared to an Alaskan Malamute or Dalmatian, Miniature Schnauzers might be considered non-shedding. This trait is one reason why some people choose the Miniature Schnauzer.

Dogs who are non-shedders are usually also thought of as being hypoallergenic (although the hairless breeds may have a leg up on being non-allergic). It is still possible, however, for people with certain allergies to react to dogs who don't shed. If your one and only reason for getting a Miniature Schnauzer is because you are allergic to dog hair, make absolutely certain before you buy one that you do not have a reaction. Visit a breeder with a lot of dogs on site, and sit down and play with them first.

Toy Schnauzers

The term "toy Schnauzer" is guaranteed to make most Miniature Schnauzer breeders a bit crazy because, according to the breed standard, no such creature as a toy Schnauzer exists. No matter what you see advertised in magazines or on websites, no toy, midsize, teacup, tiny toy, micro, or pocket Schnauzers exist, according to any breed standard.

Breeding a Miniature Schnauzer down to any size other than what has been established in the breed standard produces a dog who is not accepted in the conformation show ring. Dogs advertised as "toys" are bred so far away from the standard that they are no longer recognized by the breed clubs as being Miniature Schnauzers. If you purchase any size Schnauzer other than a Miniature, Standard, or Giant, then you will have just paid a large sum of money for an unregisterable, unrecognized dog, very much like a lovable mutt from a shelter. This is fine, as long as that is what you really want. Just be aware of what you're getting, and realize that your dog will not be eligible for registration or to participate in many activities. Additionally, these micro-sized dogs are bred down from the smallest of the small, and this miniaturization may result in negative health consequences.

True, bred-to-standard Schnauzers are available in only three sizes.. Don't let a slick-talking puppy seller convince you that a 6-pound (2.7-kg) dog is a Miniature Schnauzer. If you want a dog that small, get a Yorkie or another recognized toy breed.

WHAT'S IT LIKE TO LIVE WITH A MINIATURE SCHNAUZER?

Affectionate, loving, feisty, people-pleasing, curious, engaged, and funny, Miniature Schnauzers are true companion dogs. However, they are not the breed for everyone. This section will help you to determine whether the Mini Schnauzer is the right dog for you and your family.

A Personality-Plus People Dog

Their outgoing temperament, combined with their small size, is a prime reason why Miniature Schnauzers have been so popular for so long. Most will race up to you while you're sitting and throw their paws around your neck, as though they are hugging you.

They are indoor dogs and should not be left outside in kennels, because they need to be part of the family—they need attention.

Schnauzers are also lap dogs who want to touch and kiss you all the time. If you let them, they will sleep all night snuggled up to you in bed. Many people find the breathing sounds of a sleeping dog comforting.

Miniature Schnauzers love attention and will go almost anywhere and do almost anything with you in order to get it.

The Terrier Within

Miniature Schnauzers are real terriers who go to ground and hunt little critters. However, they are not as "terrier-ish" or dog-aggressive as some terriers can be. Miniature Schnauzers of the same sex can live together in relative harmony without having to be kept separated. In fact, they like canine companionship.

However, some caution is necessary. They don't know they're little, or at the very least, they don't care. They sometimes feel free to "tell off" bigger dogs. In short, they're feisty.

Because of their terrier personality and keen hearing, Schnauzers are self-appointed protectors of home and hearth. They make excellent alarm dogs. Even though their bark is that of a little dog, it is vociferous enough to cause true burglars to back off.

A Mini Schnauzer will alert you (by barking and running back and forth) to the presence of strangers, and he won't stop until you've faced the intruder or visitor and the dog knows that the visitor is okay. But he won't attack visitors or burglars; he limits his alarm to barking.

An Active Nature

Considered to have a moderately high energy level, Schnauzers are fairly active little dogs who must have sufficient exercise. To keep busy and to be with you, they will follow you around the house and yard, usually just a bit faster than you're going. They also enjoy time in which to lounge around as couch potatoes, totally content to sit by you or in your lap. But they are too curious, active, and intelligent to be satisfied with the life of a lounge lizard.

Car rides are a favorite activity, because your dog can watch the world go by. Visiting people they know is another wonderful way to spend time, in their opinion, especially people who dote on and fuss over them. Other favored pastimes are going for a good walk, running or jogging with you, a swim in the pool for those who like water (supervised, of course), a game of fetch, and checking out the woods or a sandy beach.

A Schnauzer will be brokenhearted if left home while you go out and have fun. After all, he is the center of the universe. These dogs don't believe for a minute that you could possibly have any fun without them, so get with their program!

They are adept at learning tricks, which is a great way to amuse both of you when the weather is bad. Even though they are not

A Breeder's Viewpoint

"Our Schnauzers love to sit on our laps, and seldom can we sit in the lounge chair without at least three of them with us," says breeder Pat Discher of Darlington, Wisconsin. "Our young dogs love to go outside; we have a fenced yard for them, and anytime we yell 'Who wants to go outside?' we get most of them.

"It is very common for several of them to try to carry out a toy in their mouths, and they have to be watched carefully or they will have half of the toys outside. They haven't learned yet to bring them back in! One thing that I notice is, if it's raining out, our older ones will practically cross their legs before they consent to going out. They look at me as though they're saying 'You want me to go out there?!!'"

Your Miniature Schnauzer will not appreciate being left behind while you go off on adventures of your own.

retrievers, they love to fetch and carry. If you train them to do so, they will put away their own toys (on command, of course, not on their own initiative). They excel at tricks that involve jumping on those strong, sturdy legs. Plus, they thrive on the positive response all dogs get when they perform tricks.

Intelligence

Schnauzers can give new meaning to the idea of a smart dog. If you don't want to live with a dog who has the distinct potential to outwit you, this may not be the breed for you. Although their intellect and basic desire to please makes them easy to train, Mini Schnauzers can also attempt to manipulate people. All dogs are masters of manipulation to one degree or another, and the smarter ones excel at it. Stay on your toes, or you may end up wondering who is training whom.

If the Mini Schnauzer decides something is going to be done a certain way, then that's the way it's going to be. For example, Schnauzers can be little dictators; some are very insistent on having their own way. They are far more persistent than most people—more than persistent, they're downright stubborn. But when that persistence is delivered with such panache, it's hard not to laugh.

It could be said that these dogs are type A personalities—except without the capacity to be an away-from-home workaholic, because home with you is exactly where they want to be. You won't be able to go to the bathroom by yourself, because you will have curious company. Where you go, they go. Some people love having a furry companion 24/7, but if you're not into constant togetherness, you might want to look for a more independent, aloof breed.

Busy and Barking About It

Schnauzers can be quite barky if not trained otherwise. Added to their energy level, the barking can be a significant problem if the owner doesn't stop it in its tracks.

They need real exercise, approximately 45 minutes a day, not just a 20-minute leashed walk around a couple of blocks. Schnauzers are bred to work all day, not to sit on the couch and eat bon-bons.

It is possible for them to be a bit too energetic, and without exercise, this problem just gets worse. If Schnauzers don't get enough exercise, they will find other outlets for their energy. Given how smart they are, the ways they find to fill their time can be destructive and alarming.

If you are not able or willing to provide a lot of exercise for the next several years, consider another breed. Remember: A tired dog is a good dog, and a good dog is often tired.

Home Sweet Home

One of the nice aspects of Miniature Schnauzers is their sheer versatility. They can adapt to living in an apartment (with plenty of outdoor exercise), a small home in the suburbs, a condo in the city, or a log cabin out in the middle of nowhere. They're wonderfully versatile and adaptable, with the exception that they should not live outside in a kennel. They must be indoors with their people, whether it's in an apartment or mansion.

If they live in an urban environment that has no yard, such as a condo or apartment, they will need more exercise than if they had a yard in which to run. They need about 45 minutes of good exercise each day. Just running around the yard isn't enough, though, so even suburbanites must make sure their dog gets enough exercise.

Often, without a human to encourage them, dogs just sniff their way around the backyard and do their "business" or lay in the sun, which is a nice way to spend some time but doesn't promote sufficient exercise. And remember: Without exercise, Schnauzers will find ways you may not like to use their stored-up energy.

Miniature Schnauzers who live in a rural area typically get a lot more exercise than do urban or suburban dogs. However, you must keep a careful eye on them to make sure that they don't run into harm's way, such as a horse corral or a face-to-face meeting with possibly dangerous wildlife.

Keeping Small Pets Safe

Because Schnauzers are true terriers, it's difficult to keep "pocket" pets such as rats, mice, and gerbils in the same house, even when caged safely. It can be done, but it takes a lot of work to keep them separated, and disasters can occur in an instant.

While certainly small enough to be portable, the Mini Schnauzer is a dog who needs to get his own exercise.

Climate Control

Miniature Schnauzers do well in all climates; they don't have problems with heat and humidity, as the flat-faced brachycephalic dogs can, and they aren't as prone to being cold, as are the low-fat sighthounds. Still, use common sense in the extremes of a season.

In the summer, don't overexercise your dog in high heat and humidity, because dogs are prone to heat exhaustion. In winter, don't go out for extended periods when it's "too cold." Too cold means different things to different dogs, even within the same breed. While jackets and sweaters can be used on little dogs like Miniature Schnauzers to trap body heat, be aware of frostbite in paws, tails, and ear tips. Most Miniature Schnauzers don't mind wearing jackets, but that doesn't mean they will automatically adjust to winter boots.

If you live in a climate where ice is common during the winter, use a pet-safe de-icer that is chemically different from the salt that is usually put out to melt ice. The real salt can harm paws. The pet-safe de-icer is more expensive but costs less than a visit to the vet clinic.

Schnauzers and Children

Miniature Schnauzers get along wonderfully with children, as long as they have a grown-up with them or the dogs have been exposed to them frequently while they were puppies. Most will come to accept children if introduced while the dog is an adult, but it's best if the dog grows up with kids. Then, they are a natural mix. Because Miniature Schnauzers are so trainable, once they understand how to act appropriately around a child, the dog and the child will love each other, and the dog will respect the child's needs.

Any dog and child interaction should be supervised by adults. Left to their own devices, trouble can develop, and the dog could end up being surrendered for adoption through no fault of his own. For example, if a child teases a dog so often that the dog becomes protective and fearful, it's not the dog's fault, but the dog pays the price. Fortunately, it's easy to forge a good relationship between children and the Mini Schnauzer. When a child learns to deal with dogs respectfully, he can use that learned respect in other relationships down the line.

Between Kids and Dogs

As soon as your puppy arrives in the house, begin to teach him to respect everyone in the family, including the children. He must be taught not to mouth, bite, or jump up. He must know that you and any child are in charge, and if the child would like to take his toy from his mouth, he should be allowed to do so without question.

Hot Weather Cautions

In hot weather, particularly when it is humid, it's harder for your dog to breathe, and his energy is sapped just dealing with the climate. Even though Miniature Schnauzers don't have the short flat face of brachycephalic dogs, such as Pugs and Bulldogs, they can still get overheated playing in the summer sun. Particularly if your Miniature Schnauzer is solid black or black and silver, curtail the hard-core exercise outside because dogs can get heatstroke, which can be fatal. Dogs don't have a body cooling system like people do, and they "sweat" in the pads of their feet.

Signs of heatstroke include body temperatures over 104°F (40°C) (normal temperature is 100°F–102.5°F [37.7°C–39.1°C]), excessive panting, dark or bright red tongue and gums, staggering, seizures, stupor, bloody diarrhea, and vomiting. Dogs can go into comas from heatstroke and possibly die. Any dog with heart or respiratory problems has a higher risk of heatstroke.

If you think that your dog is experiencing heatstroke, he needs emergency veterinary care. Try to cool him down with cool water, not ice cubes or ice water, because very cold water will constrict blood vessels and actually impede cooling. It's okay for the dog to lick ice cubes, though. Even if he appears cooled off and safe after an episode, he should still be seen by a vet immediately, because internal organs are adversely affected by high heat.

Conversely, don't allow children, yours or anyone else's, to pull tails and ears, pinch him, drop him, or scare him. Children must know that it's not acceptable to pull a dog's beard or moustache. Teasing from children is one of the worst things that can happen during a dog's formative time, so make sure it doesn't happen. If it does, nip it in the bud.

Dogs and kids are born to be companions, but that doesn't mean they should share food. Don't let your kids feed part of their dinner to your Schnauzer, and don't let your dog eat off a plate on the table—particularly a child's—because the dog will come to feel that he is alpha (or leader) over the child. If a small child tries to handfeed his leftovers to the puppy, he may find sharp puppy teeth accidentally nipping fingers instead of food.

Miniature Schnauzers can be strong-willed dogs who will cause trouble if not given proper leadership.

Exercise: A Tired Dog Is a Good Dog

Other than feeding quality nutrition and giving regular veterinary care, the best thing you can do to extend your Miniature Schnauzer's life and health is to give him plenty of heart-pumping, endorphin-causing, socially stimulating, weight-trimming, muscle-toning, blood-circulating exercise at least three or four times a week.

Exercise improves the health of bones and joints. Arthritic joints benefit from gentle, regular exercise, but if your dog is sore afterward or the next day, it might indicate the amount or type was a bit too much for him. Next time, you'll know to do less. Exercise also helps heart and lung function. It helps prevent obesity and diabetes, just as it does in people.

You don't have to participate in agility or freestyle to get enough exercise (although those are excellent approaches to physical and mental health, not to mention bonding). Long, on-leash walks of about 45 minutes are good. Off-leash exercise (and socialization), in a safe place like a fenced dog park, is also great for dogs who enjoy the company of other dogs and act appropriately toward them. Except for meals, exercise play is the best part of your dog's day. Because Miniature Schnauzers love to play fetch, you can play fetch with a stick, ball, or flying disc. If you like bicycling, your dog can run alongside you, as long as you are not going too fast and he is not afraid next to the bicycle. You can buy equipment that attaches to the bicycle but also keeps your dog a safe distance away from the moving wheels. Jogging together is also great.

Anyone is a potential friend for the extroverted Miniature Schnauzer.

Any dog who has sufficient exercise is far less likely to end up with behavior problems. If he already has behavior problems, lots of exercise goes a long way toward helping him overcome those issues.

Many Miniature Schnauzers bark too much, and lack of exercise can contribute greatly to unwanted behaviors such as excessive barking, digging, and chewing, because boredom causes dogs to find other outlets for their energy.

Given that most people don't get nearly enough exercise, it's hardly surprising that most dogs don't either. However, having a dog is one of the best reasons to get out and walk, and walking is some of the best exercise possible for both of you. Get fit and stay fit together, and your Schnauzer will reward you with better behavior and a longer life span as well.

3

PREPARING
for Your Miniature Schnauzer

Y ou have so many decisions to make when preparing for your Miniature Schnauzer! The first critical decisions are whether or not you have time for a dog, can provide financially for one throughout a long life span, and whether or not your family wants a dog (or another dog).

QUESTIONS TO ASK YOURSELF

Are you certain that your landlord or housing development will allow this dog? Do you have more pets than the zoning for your home allows? Can you really afford another pet? These questions deserve hard time and thought, and you owe it to the dog to answer them honestly. If you are a single parent with two jobs and a 10-year-old kid who wants a dog, will this work out for both of you?

Affordable?

One of the most difficult choices in your life may well end up being what to do when you have an ill or injured dog. Pet owners write to veterinary information websites regularly with such questions as "My dog was hit by a car, but I can't afford to go to the vet, so what do

Remember that the adorable puppy you can't wait to bring home will grow up into a dog who will be dependent on you for his care for many years.

I do?" or "The big dog picked up the little dog by the neck and shook him and now the little dog's eyes are whirling around. Will this stop soon? I can't afford to go the vet."

The ongoing litany of "I can't afford to take this dog to the vet" is heartbreaking. If you cannot afford to take care of a dog throughout his lifetime, don't get one. Certainly, people's financial situations have ups and downs, and income levels change. But if you feel that all you can afford is a free dog and food, this means you most likely cannot provide any dog with a good quality of life.

Miniature Schnauzers are pretty healthy dogs, particularly for such a popular breed, but every dog has medical problems. Obviously, not every dog owner can afford thousands of dollars for cancer treatment or emergency care if their dog gets hit by a car, but if you have to euthanize your dog because you can't afford a relatively inexpensive treatment, then you probably can't afford to care for any dog.

The first year of a dog's life is usually the most expensive. First, there's the cost of the puppy, vaccinations, leashes, collars, brushes, bowls, food, and basic obedience classes. Plus, most puppies usually must visit the vet for problems other than basic vaccinations, such as routine worming and well-puppy checkups.

Some people decide to save money by not going to obedience classes; sadly, a direct correlation exists between behavior and being given up at the shelter. Skipping basic obedience classes is not the best way to save money; instead, spend less on fancy equipment and toys.

Time in Your Schedule?

Lack of time is the other main reason that dogs are given to shelters or rescue groups. In today's society, people tend to rush around all the time. If everyone in your family is gone all day at work or school, and then they leave the house after dinner to participate in sports or classes, the dog is going to pay a price.

Dogs are not by nature able to be alone all day. They are social beings, need regular exercise and play, and need to go out to relieve themselves. Miniature Schnauzers require a lot of time with people. If your family doesn't have time to do these things, you may not have time for a dog. In one short, heartbreaking search, I found the following reasons given for surrendering a dog to a shelter or rescue group:

- He came to us in January at two-and-a-half years of age. His humans said they are having construction done on their home and as a result, chose not to keep him.
- This little girl's tail is upright and wagging most of the time. Despite this, her former family was no longer interested in caring for her, so she came to rescue.
- This dog is 8 years old and was surrendered because her owners worked very long hours and couldn't devote enough time to her.

Miniature Schnauzers are people-oriented by nature. They want to be with you, on you, all day, every day. While that is not reasonable or practical, they are not suited to homes that stand empty most of the time or to living outside the house in a kennel. They are smart and will be bored if left by themselves all day. Often, that boredom will manifest itself in destructive behavior.

If you are sure that you have what a dog needs, then this is a very special time in your life. Few circumstances in our lives equal the excitement of bringing home a new dog, particularly when you have been heartsick over the loss of a beloved older pet. The new dog isn't a replacement for the previous one, but rather is a successor to steal your heart and share your love.

Puppy or Adult?

Many people just assume they want a puppy, but getting an adult dog has so many benefits that the decision requires serious consideration.

The upside of puppies is that they are incredibly cute, happy,

How to Register Your Mini Schnauzer

In the United States, after you have purchased a purebred Miniature Schnauzer, you can register your pup with the AKC as long as the breeder has registered the litter. Fill out the AKC registration application form and send it in with the indicated fee. Make sure that the owner gives you a hard copy of the registration application, because you may need it if any problems crop up.

The application must be filled out together by you and the person who owns the litter (typically the breeder, but not always). The litter owner fills out most of the form, which is why the breeder usually hands it to you already completed. The litter owner answers the questions about the sex, color and markings, type of registration (full or limited), transfer date, and contact information. The application must also have the signatures of all co-owners.

You fill out the part about the dog's name (that's because you choose it) and payment information (because you're responsible for the payment). And you indicate which registration options you want. For an additional fee, you can get the Gold Registration Package, which includes a dog-care training video, an AKC pedigree for the past three generations of your dog, and a 1-year subscription to the AKC's *Family Dog* magazine. The Silver Registration package provides the three-generation pedigree, but not the video or magazine.

Register your puppy relatively soon after you get him. A late fee is charged if you don't get around to registering until a year after the litter was registered, and an even bigger late fee is imposed if you register 2 years after the litter registration date. If for some reason you didn't get the dog from the litter owner, you must fill out a Supplemental Transfer Statement for each transfer of ownership.

You can do all this online if the litter owner has already registered the litter. To register online, you need both the father's (sire) and mother's (dam) AKC registration number and your puppy's name.

In Britain, the Kennel Club offers a "Guide to Litter Registration Booklet" for information. Registering a puppy begins with the breeder, who requests to registers the litter using a "Form One." The breeder sends "Form One" and the requested fee to the KC. The KC then sends the breeder a Litter Registration Certificate and one Breeder Registration Certificate for each puppy in the litter.

When the breeder sells the puppy, the breeder signs and completes the "date of sale" part on the back of the Breeder Registration Certificate. This certificate is then given to the puppy owner. The owner must complete the Change of Ownership form and send it to the KC within 10 days. The KC then sends the new owner a Registration Certificate. Health insurance for registered dogs is available through both registries.

energetic, and full of life. Like human babies, puppies are guaranteed to elicit nurturing responses that seem independent of our will. You can't help but *ooh* and *ah* at cute puppies. And Miniature Schnauzer puppies give new meaning to the words *cute, adorable, wonderful,* and *happy.*

Nothing else in this world corresponds to the feeling you get when your new puppy snuggles up in your arms and falls asleep, trusting and content.

Also, when you get a puppy, you can train him in the way you want from the beginning. You can train him not to bark his head off. You can train him to understand that you are alpha—the leader. You know his background, and you know that no one else's mistakes have made any impact on your dog's behavior or your life with him.

Puppy Blues

Puppies require a lot of work: housetraining, obedience training, and providing sufficient exercise to burn off puppy energy. The older people get, the more energy terrier puppies seem to have. Thankfully, Miniature Schnauzers are so smart that they usually pick up housetraining quickly. That doesn't mean housetraining will happen overnight, though.

It's easy to forget how much energy a puppy has when you haven't had one for a long time. If your last dog was elderly, you might be in for a night and day kind of scenario. Having a puppy in the house is not the same as seeing a puppy at the dog park. The puppies at the dog park aren't chewing their way through your shoes or your library while they're teething. They don't need you to take them out at midnight and 4 a.m.

Some puppy tasks cannot be put off, whether you have time for them or not; for example, exercising puppies cannot be delayed without consequences. Puppies need a significant amount of exercise—Miniature Schnauzers are terriers, bred to eradicate vermin, so they are also bred for plenty of stamina and endurance. If they don't get enough appropriate exercise, they'll get plenty of inappropriate exercise on their own, usually with a low probability of making you happy.

Grown Up and Good?

The upside of adopting an adult dog is that he usually arrives housetrained, somewhat obedience trained, and is past the teething stage, which can wreak more havoc than termites. The dog's temperament is established, he's as big as he's going to get, and you'll know just how barky this particular Schnauzer is. Adopting an adult dog is, in certain respects, less of a leap of faith than adopting a puppy.

Some people mistakenly believe that deep bonding only occurs between a person and a puppy. I strongly disagree. As a matter of fact, adopted dogs know they are getting a second chance, and they usually bond to their new owners even more strongly than does a dog who hasn't known anyone else.

Part of that strong bonding is based in separation anxiety, and separation anxiety is often the downside of adopting an adult. Part of it is fear that this new home could be taken away. Whatever its cause, the depth of bonding with an adult is no less, and often more, than what you get with a puppy.

The other downside of adopting an adult is that you don't know what's happened in the dog's past to create any behavior problems. You don't know why a particular dog may have a fear of brooms, although you can guess. You probably can't guess why he loves to go for car rides but doesn't like to get in the car. Some dogs have such difficult pasts that only an experienced and compassionate trainer or behaviorist can make headway, but many of them make wonderful companions regardless.

WHERE TO FIND THE DOG OF YOUR DREAMS

Finding the right Mini Schnauzer for you requires a good deal of thought and research.

Although a beautiful stray Miniature Schnauzer is not likely to just walk up to your front door, you have many places to look for the Mini of your dreams. Breeders and Miniature Schnauzer rescue groups are a certainty, but all-breed rescue groups, shelters, and pet stores usually have Minis at one time or another. Decide what it is you're looking for (puppy, potential show dog, trained adult house pet, or a mixed-breed with obvious Schnauzer in him), and then start looking in the most appropriate places.

Breeders

Unless you are lucky enough to know someone who breeds Miniature Schnauzers, it is going to take some homework to find a dog.

If you want a puppy, your first task is to find a responsible breeder. The American Kennel Club (AKC) defines a responsible breeder as one who seeks to improve their breed with every litter. A responsible breeder does not breed to make money; most responsible breeders lose money breeding puppies.

If you definitely want a puppy—and a healthy one to share many years with you—finding a responsible breeder is your next requirement.

The best way to find a responsible breeder is to contact the national breed club and ask for referrals to Miniature Schnauzer breeders. The AKC website (www.akc.org) has an online breeder reference service, which usually gives you the phone number of the breeder referral contact for the national club, as opposed to a local club.

Breeders who participate in their local kennel clubs show an interest in the future of purebred dogs, but any individual may qualify to join a local club if that club does not have an ethics code or does not have an approval process for membership applications.

The Kennel Club offers a Puppy Sales List service that has contact information for breeders who currently have puppies available for sale. The American Miniature Schnauzer Club (AMSC) has a breeders list that offers contact information for dogs in the United States, Canada, Australia, and Mexico.

It's also a good idea to go to dog shows and talk to the people showing Miniature Schnauzers; not only will you see what the breed really should look like, but the handlers there might be able to recommend breeders.

Backyard Breeders

Finding a litter in the local newspaper is a possibility, but unfortunately, these may not be the best puppies. Often, but certainly not always, the people who run ads in the newspapers are backyard breeders, or in some cases, the owners of puppy mills.

Backyard breeders usually mean well, but many of them think "You have a registered male, I have a registered female, let's have a litter and make some money." Most backyard breeders do not participate in health evaluation or certifications, and they make no significant effort toward improving health or temperament. It's usually more of a convenience factor.

You can quickly find a puppy this way, particularly given the popularity of Miniature Schnauzers, but the puppy you buy in a hurry may have long-term issues—issues that could be avoided by going to a responsible breeder instead. Buying from a backyard breeder does not mean you're going to end up with a dog with health and temperament issues—it does, however, increase the risk.

The Responsible Breeder

A responsible breeder does not view puppies as things to be sold but as sentient beings moving from her family to yours. These breeders care very much what type of home their puppies will have and like to hear from the owners on occasion to know how things are going. Also, they want to be informed of any problems or health issues; if there's a health condition, they need to know about it for future litters.

The breeder should offer to be available to you if you have problems with your puppy. She should encourage you to call with questions.

A responsible breeder wants to know about you. The breeder is selling a little piece of her heart, and she wants to make sure that the puppy will be well treated and have a good family and permanent home. Some questions may include:

- Why do you want a dog?
- Do you have time for a dog?
- Do you have a fence?
- Who will be responsible for the dog's daily needs?
- Where will the dog spend most of his time?
- What rules will be established for the dog's behavior, such as whether or not he will be allowed on the furniture and how he is to behave with visitors?
- Can you provide a veterinary reference?
- Will you agree to neuter a pet-quality dog?
- Do you promise to return the dog to the breeder if you are unable to keep the dog for any reason?

Puppy Purchase Precautions

Use the following guidelines to help you make an informed decision when searching for the perfect puppy:

- If the seller only takes cash, run in the other direction.
- Don't buy a puppy sight unseen over the Internet or phone.
- Don't buy a puppy from someone who will not let you come to her home and see the litter.

What to Expect From the Breeder

A responsible breeder should provide documentation for the puppy in question. You should get written documentation of the exact terms to which you are agreeing with this particular breeder. Make sure that the seller has signed this documentation. Insist on seeing health certificates from both the dam and sire, such as a CERF certificate for eye health (see Chapter 8). Do not accept "Oh, that's not a problem with my line." Anyone who doesn't have a problem with the line can easily show you paperwork. And if they don't know what you mean by health certificates, they are not responsible breeders.

Get a copy of the vet records on the litter. These should include the puppy's first recorded weight from the day of birth along with such information as when the eyes opened, if the breeder gave any shots, and if so, a copy of the label on the vaccinations given by the breeder.

The puppy should not be less than 8 weeks of age before being separated from his mother and littermates to go home with you. The breeder should also let you know what vaccinations, if any, have been given by the time the puppy goes home.

Will the Breeder Take the Puppy Back?

The most critical, ethical characteristic of a breeder is whether she will take the dog back for any reason and at any time during his life. A responsible breeder wants the puppy back if you cannot keep him, as in the event of a death or other life-changing circumstances, or if the dog has aggression or medical problems you cannot manage.

It shouldn't matter why; it only matters that the breeder will take the dog back. Dogs purchased directly from breeders should not go into rescue groups if they can be returned to the breeder.

Adoption Options

Unless you plan to breed and show your Mini in conformation, it's not necessary to have a show-quality purebred with papers. If you're looking for a family pet and don't have any requirements for a dog's genetic background, adoption is a wonderful option. Many dogs in shelters and rescue care are registered purebreds who have lost their homes through no fault of their own.

Shelters

Breeders are not the only place to find purebred dogs. Shelters often have purebreds. The Humane Society of the United States (HSUS) estimates that purebreds account for about 25 to 30 percent of the dogs in shelters—that's about one in every four dogs. Given the popularity of Miniature Schnauzers, they do show up in shelters.

Some shelters offer notification to potential adopters if a breed in which you're interested arrives. Good shelters screen dogs for health and temperament issues. You can also ask if a specific dog could be "cat tested" to see if the dog can live with cats, although that's not a big concern with Miniature Schnauzers.

Some people think you can't get a good dog at a shelter, assuming the dog was taken there because he had problems. This is not typically true. Generally, people give up dogs for people-related reasons rather than dog-related reasons: no time, allergies, don't want the responsibility, got it for the kids who now won't take care of it, they haven't trained or exercised him so he's chewing door molding, or they can't afford it. Those reasons have nothing to do with whether the dog will make a good pet; they have everything to do with whether a person was a good dog owner.

Dogs who are not well behaved usually have not been trained. Someone expected to get a puppy who was born knowing how to sit and not jump up on people. Most, but not all, behavior problems stem from poor training or lack of effective leadership from the human.

Shelters provide a wonderful place for people to find dogs who deserve a second chance at a good home. Because purebreds rarely show up as small puppies at shelters, by the time a dog gets to the shelter, you can have a good idea of his adult size, appearance, and temperament.

Although separation anxiety can occur easily in a dog who is no longer with his first home, it normally can be overcome or dealt with.

Rescue

Miniature Schnauzer rescue is a wonderful place to find the dog of your dreams. Despite good intentions, sometimes it is not possible to keep a dog—owner deaths, changes in health or financial circumstances, divorce, military service, and loss of a home are some reasons people need to find new homes for their dogs. Strays may also be found in rescue.

Purebred dogs have the benefit of rescue services. People who are involved with a breed club work together to offer rescue services for a specific breed. These kind people rescue dogs from going to shelters, "free to a good home" approaches, or euthanasia.

Some Miniature Schnauzer rescue groups take mixed breeds that obviously have some Schnauzer in them. While the AMSC has guidelines for minimum rescue services, each local club has its own policies beyond those guidelines.

It is possible that you'll find the Miniature Schnauzer of your dreams through a shelter or rescue organization, where he'll have been temperament tested and evaluated for adoptability.

Rescue dogs are available for a suggested donation that covers some of the expenses taken on by the rescue group, such as veterinary care and food. Sometimes the veterinary care involved is extensive; sometimes it's only a checkup and altering. Each rescue group sets its own donation level. You can always give more than the suggested donation, of course, because rescue groups are usually in need of additional funds.

One major benefit of rescue is that the dog has already lived in a home environment and his foster parent has been able to observe temperament and health, so you can know in advance if the dog has problems with children, gets along with other dogs or cats, or has behavior problems such as separation anxiety. You may also learn in advance what type of toys he likes or if he has a food allergy. And because he is evaluated by a vet, you usually have an idea of the dog's general medical condition.

The AMSC has minimum guidelines for dogs to be placed through rescue. These services are provided by local breed clubs, but the parent club sets the following guidelines:

- Dogs are altered before adoption.
- Terminally ill dogs, or those who have bitten humans, will not be offered for adoption.
- A veterinarian checks the health of the dog prior to placement.
- All vaccinations are brought current; dogs are usually tested for heartworm.
- Dogs are groomed and kept clean.
- An adoption fee is requested to help prevent people from buying rescue dogs to use or sell for unethical purposes.
- An adoption contract must be signed for each dog; the contract must state that the dog will be returned to Miniature Schnauzer rescue if the owner cannot keep the dog for any reason.
- No AKC papers are provided to you by the rescue group.
- Where possible, existing veterinary records are given to the new owner.

The AMSC website has contact information and links to Miniature Schnauzer rescue groups. You can find these easily by searching the Internet or calling the AMSC.

Shelters often call these rescue groups if they get a Miniature Schnauzer because they know that a rescue group can take care of the dogs. In addition, usually no deadline is imposed that might result in the dog being euthanized.

Pet Stores

Some people decide to buy a Miniature Schnauzer from a pet store. Pet stores can be a convenient option, and they usually offer a wide selection of puppies. It is important to remember, though, that a dog's health, happiness, and well-being are largely dependent on his genetics and the quality of his early care. This is why you must ask the pet store to provide you with all the details of the Mini Schnauzer's breeding and history. In fact, pet store employees should be knowledgeable about dogs in general and the breeds they sell in particular.

If you are considering a Mini Schnauzer from a pet store, check the dog for any signs of poor health. A few signs of illness are nasal discharge, watery eyes, and diarrhea. A store should not be selling a dog experiencing any of these symptoms. Even if the puppy seems healthy, be sure to have him checked by your veterinarian as soon as possible. Many health guarantees offered by pet stores are contingent upon a veterinary examination within a few days of the sale.

Questions to Ask Before Purchasing a Pet-Store Puppy

You should ask some of the following questions of pet store personnel before committing to a sale:

1. *What kind of guarantee do you offer?*

   If the store only guarantees the puppy for a few hours or days but offers no compensation for future problems, such as genetic diseases, you must be aware that you will be on your own to deal with these problems. The store should be reasonably responsible for ensuring that you receive a healthy puppy.

2. *How old was the puppy when he arrived in the store?*

   Puppies taken away from their mother and littermates before 8 weeks of age are at a great developmental disadvantage. Puppies learn a lot about social interaction from their mother and littermates, and getting shipped across the country in a crate is no way to begin life as a 6-week-old puppy. Those taken away too young and exposed to these frightening experiences often develop fearful or aggressive behaviors later in life. The best-case scenario is one in which the puppy was hand-delivered by a breeder to a pet store after 8 weeks of age.

3. *Can I see the vaccination and worming record?*

   Puppies should have had at least one and preferably two sets of complete vaccinations and a worming by 8 weeks. (This depends on the breed.) The pet store should have complete documentation of this and any other veterinary care the dogs have received.

4. *Is the puppy registered?*

   Registration is no guarantee of quality, and some registries will register any dog without proof of a pedigree (a written record of a dog's lineage). Dogs who are registered with the American Kennel Club or Kennel Club may be more likely to come from breeders who are following certain standards, but it's not a guarantee. However, the AKC does at least have minimum standards for record keeping and care for large breeders.

   Some small local breeders may provide to pet stores puppies

who are unregistered but who will make healthy, fine pets. Ask about this, because it will help get the employees talking about the dog and the breeder. The more questions you ask about the store's source for puppies, the more you might find out about the breeder's priorities and history.

GENERAL HOME PREPARATION

While preparing for a dog is not as intense as preparing for a two-legged infant, there are some things you need before your Mini walks in the door for the first time. If this is your first dog, you will need to get all the supplies at once, whereas if you have had a dog or have others now, you may just need to get a new ID tag and collar for your new family member.

Once you've found your puppy, begin preparing your home for his arrival, remembering that it will be a major transition for him to leave his littermates and join your family.

When

Before your puppy sets any of those four adorable feet in his new home, set him up for success by being prepared. Avoid bringing him home for the first time during hectic, busy times, such as when you have company for holidays or a 70-member family

reunion in your backyard. It's not the holiday that's a problem, it's the extra people and confusion.

In some respects, a holiday may be a perfect time to bring your puppy home because you're not working. A nice, calm vacation without extra people in your home is a great time to welcome him, so that you have more than just a weekend together before you go back to work.

How

Even though you've been waiting for this day for months, or possibly your whole life, your puppy is not likely to be quite as pleased as you are. He has just been taken away from his mother and siblings and has gone to a new place with strangers. Everything is unfamiliar to him.

He will not like being alone at first, without his littermates. He may be frightened. However, because Miniature Schnauzers are very affectionate, he will bond quickly to you and your family. Give him a little space, don't crowd him, and let him acclimate in his own time.

Before the puppy arrives, decide who is responsible for what part of his care. Decide who feeds him, walks him, housetrains him, and so forth. If you live alone, then you have a fairly obvious answer. If there's only two of you, puppy care is easy to divvy up. Be careful when there are multiple people involved—make sure the puppy chores get done but not overdone, like feeding him five times each morning!

You should also decide before The Big Day where the puppy is going to sleep and if you're going to crate train. Where will the puppy stay when you leave the house? Have all the basic equipment, such as a crate, his own bed, food and water bowls, and a couple of toys, at the house before he arrives.

Small children will be very excited at the puppy's arrival, but take care that their excitement doesn't frighten the puppy. Show children how to properly pick up the puppy with both hands, supporting both his chest and back end, and hold him so he doesn't get dropped. Being dropped accidentally can cause a dog to be frightened forever of anything related to that incident. Also, teaching children how you want them to hold and approach a dog is safer for them and the puppy.

Puppy Proofing

All small children and puppies experience the world through physical sensations, primarily using the mouth. Your puppy will mouth anything and everything from cats to car keys to remote controls to books. Therefore, set your puppy up for success by removing from his nimble reach those items that you don't want him to have.

Close doors to rooms you don't want him in and protect your shoes in particular, because they smell like you. Remove things from his level that you know will interest him. If your collection of porcelain porcupines is on the bottom

Help your puppy feel more secure during his first few days in your home by paying special attention to him.

shelf of an open cabinet, store them somewhere else (like a closed box) until the puppy is trustworthy. If you store potentially hazardous cleaning materials, such as bleach or ammonia, within puppy reach, either move them for a few months or place a child-proof lock on the cabinet door.

Keep garbage, the contents of which have caused pancreatitis in many dogs, under tight cover, outside, or up high. Electrical cords, particularly those that nest behind a computer, are attractive to dogs and should be taped together or pulled out of the way as much as possible. It's hard to realize or remember how little it takes to attract the attention of a curious, highly intelligent, small dog.

That First Long, Cold, Fretful Night

A young puppy who has just left the other Miniature Schnauzers in his life is in for a sad first night. You wouldn't be a happy camper either, if you'd just been taken away from your family by total strangers with no explanation and no idea of what's going to happen.

Make it as easy as possible for your puppy and let him sleep in your bedroom, in a crate, or on his own dog bed placed near your bed. Leaving him in an empty room will only increase his angst. Besides, if he's sleeping near you, you'll have a much better idea of when he needs to go out, which may be more often than you think or remember from your last puppy.

It will not ruin your dog's temperament to let him sleep in your bed, and it won't make him some kind of tyrant who thinks he runs the household. He's either an alpha dog or he isn't, and sleeping in your bed isn't going to make a difference. As a matter of fact, he will find this more comforting than anything in the world on that first night, and it's a terrific way for you to bond to each other.

Miniature Schnauzers are barnacles with mustaches. They will glue themselves onto your body. No matter where he sleeps though, you want him to learn that he has his own space, preferably a crate that he will always view as his personal place. Just remember that, until he's older and fully housetrained, if he sleeps outside of a crate, he may have bladder-control issues. You probably won't be too excited about a 3 a.m. "accident" on your pillow, so you might want to wait until housetraining is completed before letting him sleep in your bed with you.

Websites and Puppy Mills

Responsible breeders do not offer contracts for puppies to the general public sight unseen. Responsible breeders assure themselves first that their babies are going to good, caring homes, and they will interview you first, often at length.

If you find puppies available on websites that advertise things like "print your contract here" or "give us your Miniature Schnauzer deposit by clicking here," you are not dealing with a reputable breeder. Many mass producers of puppies, often referred to as puppy mills, have websites that are designed to make them look like they are a reputable breeder.

If you are going to spend the money for a purebred dog, buy a well-bred one who will be healthy and happy, and is more likely to make you happy over the 14 or so years this Miniature Schnauzer will be in your life and home. With a puppy-mill dog, you will spend more at the vet than you would ever have spent buying a well-bred puppy in the first place. Also, some of those temperament issues like human aggression, dog aggression, or fear, which should never occur in a well-bred Miniature Schnauzer, are issues that can make your life difficult.

It is understandable that you want to get a dog as soon as you decide the time is right, but buying a dog is one area where impulse purchases have a long-term negative impact. Use your head more than your heart when you start your search for your Miniature Schnauzer.

SUPPLIES

Miniature Schnauzers don't need more than any other kind of puppy does. The world on a platter will do fine. Okay, maybe not quite that much.

Bed

Your puppy will need a collar that is the correct size and weight and that fits comfortably and securely.

Even if your dog will sleep with you in your bed, it's nice for him to have his own bed. Despite their usual preference for glomming onto people, there are times when every dog likes to nap quietly by himself. If another dog is annoying them, or there is too much noise elsewhere in the house, or if they don't feel well, they may want to go to their own bed. If you have a crate with a pad in it, this could be used as a bed, or you could have one located outside of the crate.

Personally, I prefer a bed that can be washed in warm water so that stains and odors from urine, chew treats, food remnants, vomit, and even medicated ointments wash out more thoroughly. While Miniature Schnauzers do not shed, there will still be a bit of hair on the bed, so choose a model that can also go in the dryer for better fur removal.

Food and Water Bowls

Plastic bowls can harbor bacteria and can be chewed, so ceramic or metal ones are usually a better choice. Wash any water bowl frequently with dishwashing soap because eventually the bowl becomes scummy. You may want to have a placemat underneath the two bowls, although it's not necessary—just neater. The facial hair of a Miniature Schnauzer can spread water around a bit.

Collar and Leash

Your puppy needs a collar and leash. The variety of matched sets is a lot of fun to choose from, and you can easily find a collar that suits your dog. A soft adjustable collar is the best way to start, one with a buckle or break-away fastener. For a puppy, choose a lightweight set so that less weight drags on the neck. (Chain link leashes are too heavy for puppies.) Buy a leash that is 4 to 6 feet (1.2 to 1.8 m) in length.

Slip collars can be effective in training, but only if they are used correctly. If used incorrectly they become *choke collars*. This type of collar is not used by positive reinforcement trainers because of the physical discomfort it causes—a negative approach to training. Miniature Schnauzers can be dubious about training, and they do best with positive reinforcement. Typically, inexperienced owners do not know how to use slip collars correctly. Incorrect use can cause injury to a puppy's soft neck. If you choose to use this type of collar, make sure that a knowledgeable person shows you how to use it properly, because it is not as simple as it appears.

Crate

You don't absolutely *need* a crate, but it can make life significantly safer for your puppy and easier for you. A crate gives your dog a place to call his own, a place where he feels totally safe.

Fencing

No single other tool is as effective for your dog's ongoing safety as a fence. Other dogs, wildlife, children, and people are not allowed to enter into your dog's area without your permission. The fence keeps your dog inside a specific perimeter, unless he's a digger. All terriers—who by definition go to earth—have the potential to dig. Some terriers will dig and some won't, but for those dogs who do, you must check the base of the fence on a regular, preferably daily, basis. I once looked out the front window and saw my dog, who had just been in the backyard, trotting down the street (hence the need for identification on your dog's body).

Electronic fences are not ideal because they do not keep out other dogs or wildlife. If your dog runs to get away from a dog who has entered the electronic fence perimeter, your dog faces a choice of being cornered or being zapped. Also, the electronic notification that makes the fence work, the "zap," can be mentally detrimental to some sensitive dogs, and you may find a change in temperament that you don't like. However, in some communities, private fences are not allowed, or the ground is too rocky and uneven; in these cases, an electronic fence is better than having no fence at all.

Miniature Schnauzers are, by nature, people-oriented dogs and will be very unhappy if forced to live outside in the yard. They like to play in a yard, but they do best if they live in the house.

Many people with multiple dogs feed their dogs in their crates, both to reinforce happy things in the crate and to keep the dogs separated at meal times. It is a huge boon to housetraining, because a dog never wants to soil the spot where he sleeps or eats. And if your dog ever needs to rest after surgery, crates are an excellent place to do so as long as he's already accustomed to it. If you crate your puppy when you leave the house, you will not return to find the aftereffects of a puppy tornado, or a puppy sick from chewing inappropriate items. Being in the crate means he won't be able to pull books off a shelf and hit himself in the head or go for a third helping of door molding. While Miniature Schnauzer puppies are much smaller than Great Dane puppies, don't underestimate the damage a small, curious puppy can do.

Using crates for traveling, either to earthdog tests or your mother's house, is a plus. Fiberglass kennels are good for air travel, but for home and car use, wire mesh crates allow better air ventilation than do the fiberglass crates.

Be careful that your dog does not spend too many hours a day in a crate. Crates can be excellent training tools, but dogs shouldn't be in a crate all day while you're at work and then again while you sleep. That's too much time in a crate, especially if you also crate him while you run to the grocery store. Behavioral problems can crop up as a result of too much time in a crate, so try not to overdo a good thing.

Grooming Supplies

Basic grooming supplies include a wire slicker brush, metal comb, trimming scissors, nail trimmers, and styptic powder. (See Chapter 5 for a full list of grooming equipment.)

Toys

Toys are not just for fun. They're quite necessary, particularly when your puppy is teething and the only thing he wants in the world is to relieve the discomfort in his jaw by clamping down hard on something about six thousand times a morning. To ensure that he's not chomping on your shoes, get him a few toys. Don't get every toy in the store, because having too many to choose from is almost as bad as not having any. Variety is good, but only add to the stockpile over time.

Toys help puppies develop into adults. As with human children, playtime boils down to practice for real life. Play fighting, hunting, and chasing help the puppy grow up. Playing with toys also helps develop muscle tone and creativity (not that you necessarily want your Miniature Schnauzer to be more creative; they're pretty creative as it is—it's one of those areas where you can have too much of a good thing).

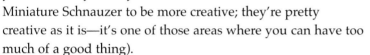

Beyond the fun factor, toys are necessary for your puppy's physical and mental development.

Rubber toys are good for teething puppies, but they also love squeaky fleece toys. As vermin eradicators, Miniature Schnauzers like to "kill" toys and can fling them in the air with wild abandon. Chasing after rolling balls improves motor skills.

Not to be forgotten, when you and your dog play—with or without toys—you bond together. Because you are in control of the games, you also reinforce your status as leader of the pack. Playing with toys also helps teach mouth inhibition, which every puppy must learn to prevent nipping.

Safety Gates

Depending on the setup of your home, a safety gate designed for pets (or babies) can be a useful tool. You can block off rooms where you don't want the dog to go, such as a nursery or office, but he can still see in. Or you can keep the dog in one room, such as the kitchen.

Gates can be used to block off stairs so that your dog doesn't fall down the steps. Many people use them to block a dog's access to a cat's litter box.

Some gates are designed with a built-in doorway, so that you can go through it without removing or stepping over the gate. Many styles and widths are available. Check places that sell either pet supplies or baby supplies. Safety gates are a worthwhile investment.

Spot Removers and Other Cleansers

In dog talk, spot removers are meant to remove the spots dogs leave when they throw up or pee or poop inside. (Dogs consider brand new, light-colored carpeting to be a proper place for these activities.)

If the scent of any urine or feces is left, the dog will return to a spot to do it again and again. Through the years, my many dogs have repeatedly hit one spot on the top of the carpeted stairwell, as though a sign is posted that says "Vomit Here" with an arrow pointing to the corner of the landing. I eventually put in new carpeting, but it didn't take long before it was "christened" again. Even the cat leaves hairballs there.

White vinegar helps reduce the stain left by urine spots, but it's usually not quite enough to remove all odor in carpets. You can buy a product specifically designed for cleaning pet spots on carpeting, and enzyme cleaners are available that really kill the scent. Keep the cleaner within easy reach until you're through with housetraining.

If you eradicate the scent immediately, you'll have far less trouble in the future, whether the spots are on carpeting, tile, or hardwood floors. Once the padding below the carpeting is ruined, it's almost impossible to get dogs to stop peeing in that spot.

It takes years of dedication and involvement to recognize the best qualities of a purebred Min Pin.

Identification

Sometimes, no matter how careful you are, your dog will get out. He will dig under the fence, jump through the electronic fence, or knock out a window screen while barking at the neighbors who have the effrontery to walk their dog past his house. Dogs new to a house, particularly adults, are prone to bolting out the door. It can be a terrifying experience, especially if you live in a busy area. Whatever the reason, Miniature Schnauzers are smart enough to figure a way out if they want out. You might say they're *really* persistent. It's best to be prepared in case the unexpected happens. There are several ways to place identification on your dog so that he can be returned to you after he goes out on some kind of Australian walkabout, communing with nature and Interstate 80.

Tags

First and foremost, each dog should have an ID tag on his collar. Some cities require that the dog wear an ID tag along with a rabies tag and city license at all times. A tag should provide your phone number and the dog's name, at the very least. Some people put their addresses on, some don't; some swear by the use of "Reward" on the tag. The problem with tags is that they can become disconnected from the collar, or the dog may lose the whole collar. But having them is still a good bet.

I once came home to find a phone message saying "We have your dogs, come and get them." I called and said, "There must be some mistake because my dogs are here." The woman said, "I know, we're so close that we walked them home. The gray one was easy, but that tan one…" The whole episode was over before I knew it had begun, and my dogs got home because of the address on their tags.

Microchipping

Microchipping has improved over the years, thanks to the advent of scanners that usually can detect the presence of other manufacturers' chips. In the early days of microchip use, two companies existed, and each one used a different scanner. Most shelters could only afford one, so the chance of the shelter being able to scan your dog's chip was only 50-50. These days, that's not a problem, and chipping is a better option.

Your veterinarian implants the chip under the skin between the shoulder blades, using what looks like a big syringe. Microchips are inserted in the same place in each dog so that people know where to place the scanner. No local anesthesia is needed. After insertion, your vet checks that the chip works using a scanner.

You send in your information along with the chip's specific number to the company that made the chip, as well as payment to register the information, and you're on file. It's a one-time payment, not an annual fee. The company puts the chip number

Mini Schnauzer Supplies

You'll need the following items when you bring your new Mini Schnauzer home:

- bed
- collar and leash
- crate
- grooming supplies
- identification
- safety gates
- spot removers and other cleansers
- toys

associated with your dog into a database. If you move or change phone numbers, notify the company so that your records can be updated. Should your dog get away, shelters can scan your dog, call the database, and find you. The good part about microchips is that they can't be lost. The bad part is that, without a scanner to read them, they are useless. Plus, not everyone thinks to bring a lost dog to a shelter or vet to see if he's been chipped. A microchip provides additional protection to an ID tag; it doesn't replace it.

Tattooing

Tattooing isn't quite as common as it used to be, but it is still used. Typically, it's done on show dogs as an added safety precaution. Many breeders have tattoo kits and tattoo their own dogs.

Before credit fraud was rampant, many people used their social security number as the tattoo. In this day and age, that could be unwise. Drivers' license numbers can also lead to fraudulent use if "borrowed." In place of those numbers, many people use either the dog's AKC registration number or an identification number from a company that provides tattooing services.

WHEN YOU'RE GONE

Your dog might be offended at the very thought that you would leave town for vacation and not take him. But there are many times and circumstances in which you need someone else to take care of your pets, such as a vacation where pets aren't allowed, a business trip, or an emergency trip, such as for a funeral.

Your best bet is to find someone to watch your dog or to find a place to leave him before you need it. If your vet's clinic doesn't board, ask them if a good kennel exists in the area. People seem to have a harder time with the concept of kennels than dogs do, and many dogs think of going to the kennel as going to camp. One way to identify a good kennel is to ask if it is accredited with the American Boarding Kennels Association.

Professional pet sitters are another option, particularly if you have more than one pet. They should be bonded (legally trustworthy) and insured. They can stay at your house or drop by for a pre-assigned number of visits per day, typically two or three. Often, vet techs or other people who work at your clinic and already know your dog are willing to housesit for a fee.

Perhaps a friend or relative you trust can take care of your pets, and they can stay at your home. *Trust* is the operative word. Think twice about having a teenager or college student stay. Make absolutely sure that they are responsible enough to take good care of your pets and not let them get lost, and that they will be home enough to take care of them.

In all these scenarios, make certain that whoever is in charge understands your dog's needs, any medications, any medical problems, and how to reach you in case of an emergency. A pet sitter told me that a couple she sat for frequently once left town in a hurry for a funeral and forgot to leave a phone number; while they were gone, their 20-year-old cat died and the pet sitter had no way to contact them. Don't let this happen to you.

TRAVELING WITH YOUR DOG

Many people prefer to travel with their Miniature Schnauzers rather than leave them behind. They usually make excellent traveling companions, provided you use common sense and are adequately prepared.

First, follow the rules of common courtesy and ask before you bring your dog(s). It is not cool to show up for a weekend at a friend's house with a dog in tow if you haven't asked first—some people frown on having dogs in their home, even incredibly cute, cuddly little gray lap dogs with big mustaches. (I know—they're crazy, but what can you do? It's their house.)

Miniature Schnauzers are wonderful travel companions who will eagerly join you on the road.

While there, make sure your dog does not bother anyone by barking, taking over the couch, gardening the prize roses, or terrifying the family guinea pig who, after all, got there first. Perhaps your friend's ancient mother-in-law is afraid of dogs because she was bitten by one when she was four; show her fear some respect. Traveling is a good time to remember that not everyone likes dogs, much less sleeps with four of them plastered to their body.

If you intend to stay at a motel, check a travel guide to see which motels or hotels accept dogs. Places that accept dogs usually say so on their outdoor

signs. Rules are rules, and just because you're stuck in an ice storm doesn't mean they're going to change their policy for you.

At places that are nice enough to allow dogs, be thoughtful and don't make it hard for other dog owners down the road. While you're gone, don't let your dog bark in the room and annoy other guests. Pick up after your dog, inside and out, and clean up the carpet if any accidents occur. This is your responsibility, not the motel's. If you leave the dog in the room, hang out the "do not disturb" sign so that employees are not startled and there's less chance your dog will get out.

If you are going to a dog show or competition, make sure you pick up after your dog and only let him go in designated areas. Venues for dog shows can be hard to find, and common courtesy and cleanliness go a long ways toward how venue operators feel about allowing future dog shows.

Before you leave for your travels, check your dog's identification to see that the information is current and that the ID tag is in good shape.

By Car

If you're driving, think about how to keep your dog safe. Many people drive with their dogs in a crate. It keeps them contained in event of an accident, so that they don't become doggy projectiles, and it keeps them from crawling into the front seat or stepping on the power window button. Other people prefer seat restrainers, a type of doggy seat belt. If the car has front or side air bags, the dog is safest in the back seat.

It can't be said often enough: Don't leave your dog alone inside a car when it's hot. The temperature can shoot up to dangerous levels quickly, and dogs can go into heat distress while you're in the grocery store for a few minutes. Even with all the windows cracked, temperatures inside a closed car can reach a deadly 120°F (38.8°C) in only a few minutes. It's a preventable disaster. Conversely, if you're driving in winter, you can leave the dog in the car alone for a few minutes, but not too much longer. Stop every couple of hours for a quick potty break. Carry fresh water with you. Some people carry bottled water from home with them, so that the dog doesn't get digestive upset from a change in water.

Doggy Day Care

It may sound silly to your grandfather, who wouldn't pay a penny to have someone watch his dog while he was at work, but doggy day care is growing rapidly in popularity. If you work long hours, doggy day care is a great way to get your dog exercised, intellectually stimulated, and socialized while you work.

Like children's day care, all doggy day care facilities are not created equal. Do your homework. Good ones will only take dogs with acceptable temperaments; if a dog-aggressive dog starts a fight in the middle of a room with 50 dogs of uncertain temperament, a free-for-all could result, with unhappy consequences.

Visit the doggy day care centers in your area and look around. Do the dogs look stressed out? Is there a formal limit on how many dogs they can have on a certain day? Is there sufficient space? Are there messes in the middle of the floor? How big is the exercise area? Are there enough toys to go around? Do you like the people working there?

With a little research, you can feel comfortable with your choice and come home from a bad day at work to pick up a dog who has already had a full day and isn't waiting for you to take him for a long walk in the rain.

By Air

Each airline has its own regulations about pet travel, so check with them before you make the reservation. Pet regulations change with alarming speed, even faster than meals and snacks. Regardless if you just flew with a dog 3 months ago on the same airline, check the regulations again before you go.

Ask the airline what you need. It's more than an inconvenience to show up at the airport and realize you can't go because you're not in line with some new regulation. Most airlines request a health certificate signed by a veterinarian and issued within 10 days of travel (keep your return date in mind) and a current rabies certificate. Ask what kind of crates they accept and what kind of paperwork is needed. Typically, airlines require plastic-sided crates with carrying handles, and they will not accept wire or fabric crates.

The crate should have enough room so that your dog can stand up and turn around. The bottom should be lined with absorbent material. Put a visible sticker on the outside of the crate, showing pertinent information, such as your name and address, a LIVE ANIMAL sticker, an arrow designating "this end up," the destination, and a phone number at your destination. Some Miniature Schnauzers, especially puppies, are small enough to fly in the cabin with you, as long as the crate fits under the seat in front of you. When booking your flight, ask specific questions about the size and type of carrier you can use. Some airlines allow soft, flexible crates in this circumstance.

4

FEEDING
Your Miniature Schnauzer

N utrition is a critical component of your dog's life. Providing quality nutrition helps keep your Mini healthy, happy, and out of the vet's office. The better your dog's nutrition is and the more you understand it, the better his life will be.

YOUR FEEDING RESPONSIBILITIES

It's not your imagination. Some dogs really will eat anything whether or not it's good for them: cardboard, broken glass, asparagus, espresso, pantyhose, ravioli, poop (frozen or not), string beans, cotton, string, and so on. That's because dogs are omnivores. True to their nature, dogs are not discriminatory and will eat things like a 10-day-old tuna sandwich left out on a Florida porch in July. Even other dogs' vomit is seen by some dogs as a treat.

It is up to you to monitor what goes into your dog's mouth, although with some Miniature Schnauzers, this comes under the category of easier said than done. It may take vigilance, it may take padlocks, but you're up to the challenge, or at least you will be after the first time you come home to find that your dog has vomited tonight's roast pork and carrot cake on your mother-in-law's antique couch.

COMING HOME

The first day you bring your Miniature Schnauzer home is no time to change the food he's been eating. There's enough excitement going on, and a change in food could produce digestive upset and subsequent accidents that add to the stress of major life change. Diarrhea can result from a change in food given too quickly, even without the stress of a new home.

Before you walk out from wherever it is that you get your new dog—puppy or adult—ask what the dog has been eating, and make sure you stick with that for a while until the newness of your home has worn off, say for a week or two. Then, if you want, feel free to slowly change over to whatever it is you intend to feed.

READING THE LABELS

Pet food is regulated through many sources. In the United States, it is regulated by the Federal Drug and Food Administration, the Association of American Feed Control Officials (AAFCO), and the U.S. Department of Agriculture. In addition, some states have state-specific feed and labeling laws.

The AAFCO is an organization composed of government people

Wherever you go with your dog, make sure to bring a bowl and lots of cool, clean water.

responsible for creating and executing regulations regarding animal feed. This association defines ingredients that can be used in pet food, establishes nutrition profiles, and conducts feeding trials.

Look for the phrase "complete and balanced" on pet-food packaging—the AAFCO has defined appropriate nutrition for a canine diet, and the pet food manufacturer has conducted feeding trials to make sure its food meets the AAFCO's definition.

Read the label on any pet food to see what's actually in there. It's amazing what you can learn. For some reason, in the United States, the legal requirements for pet food labeling are stricter than they are human food labeling. So, while you may have trouble deciphering what's in your dinner, you can more easily see what's in the dog's bowl.

The "Guaranteed Analysis" offered on commercial foods is required by law. It refers to the values, usually either the minimum or maximum, of nutrients. Typically, you'll see a minimum level of protein and fat and a maximum of other materials such as fiber and water. By-products, by the way, can contain some food-animal parts that people don't eat, so by-products go straight to the pet food manufacturers. It is critical to understand what is meant by "flavoring." If the label of ingredients starts with chicken, the food must be at least 3 percent chicken. If the label says it has chicken flavoring, then it only must have enough chicken flavor for dogs to detect the taste. (Given the capacities of the canine nose, dogs can detect a chicken scent at 300 paces.) But flavoring doesn't mean actual chicken is in the food. Flavored food is not as nutritious as the kind that actually contains meat.

A high-quality kibble should form the basis of your Mini Schnauzer's diet.

Feed Me, Seymour!

Even though they are not in the Hound group, Miniature Schnauzers are food hounds. They will look up at you balefully with those huge brown eyes, nose quivering, making silent or not-so-silent requests for more food. It's like a canine version of Oliver Twist: "Please, sir, may I have some more?"

You Mini Schnauzer will indicate to you that he is starving to death and that the room is spinning and turning dark, and he will die (or at least pass out) if you don't give him some of your lasagna right this second. He will use the same approach to get you to move dinner time up by 15 minutes each day, so that eventually you are serving dinner at 11:30 a.m.

Do not fall prey to this manipulation. Dogs are masters at the food game, and Miniature Schnauzers are no exception. Some are worse than others. When it comes to the ability to focus, there's nothing in this world like a dog directing his attention toward food you have that he wants.

Your Mini will practically turn somersaults to get you to give him more food than he needs. Most dogs, like many people, do not differentiate between need and want. Some dogs can self-regulate their food intake, but many are completely clueless and suffer from tunnel vision in which food, not light, is at the end of the tunnel.

Be firm, be in charge, be the alpha who knows that a lot of extra tidbits here and there are too much of a good thing. Think of it as though you were to eat nothing but chocolate: It sounds appealing in the beginning, but it doesn't work out well over the long haul.

Just say no.

FOOD CHOICES

Whatever your dog's food preferences, and whatever medical conditions your Mini has, the right food is available. Read labels, just as you do for your own food, so that you can make informed choices.

Kibble

Most people opt to feed commercially prepared dog food called *kibble*. It is convenient to use and travel with. Given the wide range of quality in kibble, it's best to use a higher-priced, quality, or premium food. Premium foods tend to be more nutritious than are inexpensive brands. Some kibble appears to be little more than filler. Read the label to find out exactly what you're buying.

Premium food may seem more expensive at first, but your dog will be healthier on it and will be less likely to have medical problems—in the long run, you may spend less time and money on veterinary care. Premium food is the best way to go. You wouldn't feed your two-footed kids nothing but fast food, would you?

Canned Food

Having canned dog food every day is a bit like having a daily ice cream sundae with chocolate and caramel sauce, at least in terms of calorie and fat content. Canned food also has a significant water content.

Semi-Moist Food

Moist food for dogs is the nutritional equivalent of junk food. While it might be fun for a treat once in a while, don't base your Schnauzer's diet on this mostly artificial stuff—it has far too much salt and sugar for daily use.

Home-Cooked Food

Some people choose to cook their dog's food at home. Many of these people choose to do this because the dog has some food allergies, but often it is motivated by devotion and a desire to make the dog happy. It's not hard to prepare a diet that is nutritionally acceptable. Talk to your veterinarian or a veterinary nutritionist to see what is appropriate for your Schnauzer. Ingredients may change depending on health conditions. Books are available on the subject, so do some research.

Don't let your dog eat cooked bones, because they may splinter and rupture his esophagus or intestines.

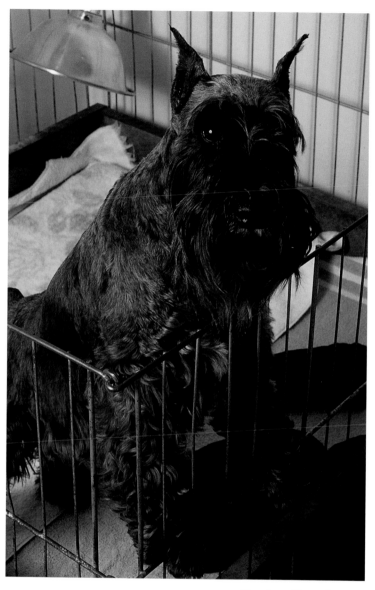

Your dog will soon learn the sound of the refrigerator door opening and will want to know what you're getting in there for him.

Table Scraps

While given with love and the best of intentions, table scraps are bad for dogs. They are full of grease, fat, and spices, not to mention some foods that are not easily digestible by canines. It is so tempting to make your dog happy by giving him your leftover pizza or pancakes, but those calories add up really fast. Also, some dogs learn to prefer people food to the point where they refuse to eat dog food. Then you are facing a whole new kettle of inedible worms.

Raw Diet

A raw diet is often referred to as a biologically appropriate raw food (BARF) diet. Controversial among veterinarians, the raw food diet essentially consists of raw meat and bones, chicken or beef organs, and green leafy vegetables. Sometimes, the vegetables, bones, and portions of the meats may be pureed together in a food processor. Bones should always be fed with caution, because a possibility of choking, puncture, or blockage exists.

Feeding raw is more complicated than just mixing together some uncooked ingredients, so if you are considering starting this diet, do some significant research. The proper calcium/phosphorus ratio must be maintained. Meat without bones is insufficient, so you can't just feed raw hamburger. The diet is easy to prepare, and advocates swear by the health of their dog, but you must know what you're doing.

Professional dental cleanings are often unnecessary with this diet, because the raw bones clean the teeth beautifully. Because no filler is eaten, the volume of poop is smaller and the pieces disintegrate quickly, making for easier cleanup.

One controversy with raw diets is over possible bacteria

Every dog is different and has unique nutritional needs. An active Miniature Schnauzer, like this one, could benefit from carefully chosen supplements.

and parasites in the uncooked meat. Those who dislike it think the bacteria causes health problems. In response to the claims of some that it's natural for the dog, who would eat raw meat in the wild, other people counter that the meat people buy at the butcher shop is not natural, because the animals have been given antibiotics and other drugs that wild prey would not have ingested.

Make your own informed decision. If you choose to start feeding raw, do your research and understand what the diet really is. Don't just start throwing raw chicken backs and some whizzed-up spinach and red lettuce at your dog. Read books by such people as Ian Billinghurst, DVM, Wendy Volhard, and Kymythy Schultze.

Toxic Foods

Dogs should not be given certain foods because they are toxic to the species or can cause digestive problems. They include the following:

- Alcohol
- Caffeine
- Chocolate: Can cause cardiovascular difficulties and seizures, diarrhea and vomiting, hyperactivity; dark chocolate is the most dangerous
- Garlic: Far less toxic than onions and often healthful in small quantities, but a potential problem for dogs with hemolytic anemia when ingested in large quantity
- Grapes and raisins: Large amounts can cause acute kidney failure
- Macadamia nuts: Substances in the nuts can cause movement difficulties; however, the information about macadamia nuts is a little sketchy—some dogs react to a couple of macadamia nuts, while others can eat half a jar of chocolate-covered macadamia nuts without ill effect
- Moldy food
- Onions or onion powder: Onion toxicity can cause hemolytic anemia
- Potatoes, particularly when they're still green
- Salt
- Xylitol: An artificial sweetener found in products such as gum, mints, and candy
- Yeast dough

Commercial Raw Diets

Enough interest exists in raw diets that some businesses offer prepared raw pet food diets. Typically, the food is organic and comes ready to be mixed with meat you provide. Some products— even frozen ones—can be conveniently shipped right to your door. You don't need to worry about proportions or whether or not you're providing a balanced diet. These diets are rather expensive, though, and so are more reasonable in cost for a Miniature

Schnauzer than a German Shepherd. The company selling the food provides information about portion size.

Vegetarian Diets

Dogs are not biologically well suited to be vegetarians. While technically they are omnivores (who eat everything and anything), they are essentially carnivores, who need to eat meat.

Prescription Diets

Some medical conditions require a change in diet. Kidney trouble often means that the dog should have food lower in protein. Liver diseases can mean the dog might need less fat or protein, while other conditions require higher or lower amounts of sodium.

Diabetic dogs need an absolutely consistent amount of nutrition and carefully regulated portions of protein and carbohydrates. Gastric problems need food that is bland and easy to digest.

Prescription diet kibble is only available through veterinary clinics for good reason: It is fed by prescription only. You don't want to diagnose a problem on your own, feed something lower in protein because you think it's the kidney, and then discover it's not a kidney problem at all. If your Miniature Schnauzer has a medical condition that can be aided by a prescription diet, your veterinarian will tell you.

SUPPLEMENTS

Supplements are nutritional ingredients that are supposed to help improve diet or health. Healthy adult dogs and puppies shouldn't need supplements, although some situations may be benefited by supplementation. Arthritic dogs usually benefit from glucosamine and chondroitin. If your younger dog had a traumatic injury that affected a joint, these supplements may be helpful well before seniorhood.

Dogs who have regular trouble with constipation may benefit from fiber or psyllium husks. Fiber can be given as a bit of bran cereal. Psyllium husks come in a powder form and should be mixed with something, such as canned food. Rather than buying an over-the-counter product for people at the drug store, you can buy psyllium husks for a much better price at health food stores. Ask your veterinarian how much of this type of product to give your Miniature Schnauzer; approximately 2 tablespoons of psyllium is needed for a 20-pound (9.1-kg) dog.

Dogs with coat or skin problems such as allergies benefit from omega-3 and omega-6 fatty acids, fish oil, flaxseed oil, and vitamin E. On product labels, the omegas are often referred to as *essential fatty acids*. Many products with essential fatty acids are on the market. Brewers yeast can help the skin conditions of some dogs with allergies, but not all (as is true with most supplements). Brewers yeast has protein, zinc, and biotin.

If your dog is recovering from a major medical event, such as cancer treatment, or has an ongoing chronic condition like diabetes, supplements may help. Ask your veterinarian which supplement would most benefit your dog's condition. Supplements you can buy at the vet clinic are usually of higher

Food is a great motivator and comes in handy at training time.

quality but cost more. If money is an issue—as it is for most of us—consider giving the higher quality supplements at times of significant medical need and less expensive ones at less critical times.

Senior dogs may benefit from supplements, the most basic of which is a vitamin and mineral pill. Antioxidants like vitamins C and E may be helpful in slowing down the aging process. Antioxidants help neutralize free radicals, which can be harmful; they protect the body's cells and tissues from damage. Many veterinarians specializing in geriatrics recommend antioxidants after the breakdown in aging body systems begins, after which antioxidants should be continued for life.

TREATS

Eating too many treats, particularly without sufficient exercise to burn them off, is the fastest way for any dog to gain weight, whether the dog is a Mastiff or Miniature Schnauzer. When your dog is a puppy and has a high metabolism because he's a perpetual motion machine, he burns an awful lot of calories. He can handle the treats you give him in training class without much adjustment.

But as he grows into adulthood, you must take into account how many calories are in those treats and adjust for them in his total daily food intake. Your Schnauzer can't count the calories—and wouldn't even if he could—so it's up to you, the one who doles them out, to account for his overall intake.

Some treats are the doggie equivalent of junk food. Some are nutritious. The difference between dried liver and rawhide is significant. Dried liver has nutritious calories. Rawhide is very high in fat, which is a leading contributor to pancreatitis. Miniature Schnauzers are prone to pancreatitis (see Chapter 8), so give rawhide sparingly, if at all. Rawhides are also a potential choking hazard and can easily become a foreign object that must be surgically removed from the intestines.

Those green scented dental chews are high in calories. While daily use will do wonders for dog breath, they could have a bad influence on weight. Some dogs have a bad digestive reaction to them, while others have no trouble at all.

Miniature Schnauzers are just that—miniature. With an average weight range of 11 to 20 pounds (5.0 to 9.1 kg), it doesn't take a lot of calories to go over the daily allotment. Use treats sparingly, and account for them in your dog's daily food portions.

Training Treats

Not to be confused with the treats you give your darling just for fun, training treats are potent motivators. Because most Miniature Schnauzers are food hounds, they respond well to treats: "If you really want this piece of freeze-dried liver dangling from my fingertips, you will do as I ask. Sit boy!" Your dog will then most likely park his behind for a piece of freeze-dried liver, and might even do a cartwheel for a piece of doggie jerky.

What works best for training is something that stinks—in other words, something that smells good to a dog, can be broken into tiny pieces for multiple treats, chewed quickly, and isn't junk food.

Variety is important here. No matter how much he likes Treat A, your dog will also enjoy some of Treat B and Treat C, and may go directly into the instructor's tote bag to get some of Treat D. (Be sure to apologize even if she's laughing.) Since your goal here is motivation, variety and odor are both useful in choosing training treats.

Try to find something with more than a modicum of nutrition in it, and try to avoid the equivalent of junk food. The need for good nutrition doesn't end at maturity. String cheese works well, as does pieces of meatballs (messy but effective), liver you've cooked, little slices of hot dog, tiny pieces of low fat cheese, and so on.

Chewing can take up too much time during training, so a hard cookie or biscuit can take longer than you want and break concentration. A treat that your dog doesn't get outside of training class is a great motivator.

During basic obedience classes in puppyhood, and during classes for performance activities such as agility or advanced obedience, training treats are a necessity, not a luxury. However, just because your Schnauzer is burning some calories doesn't mean he's burning off all the extra calories he's getting in rewards, so you need to account for these calories in his daily allotment.

If you feel that you cannot lessen the amount of treats because of the amount of training you are doing, then lessen the calorie content in the treats and add more exercise. Obesity is just as bad for dogs as it is for people, and Miniature Schnauzers are happy to gobble up anything they can. Keeping an eye on their weight will help you keep them with you for many more years.

FEEDING SCHEDULES AND AMOUNTS

Different stages in the canine life cycle require different food. Seniors won't do well on the extra protein in puppy food, and overweight Minis won't do well on high-fat, high-calorie food. As your dog's needs changes, be prepared to adjust his food accordingly.

Puppies

Puppies burn a lot of calories just growing, not to mention the calories they burn while playing. They need almost double the nutrients—calories, protein, vitamins, and minerals—of an adult

Milk

Adult dogs and even some puppies can be lactose-intolerant, just like some of your friends. That means they don't have the right digestive enzyme, called lactase, with which they can break down the sugar that occurs naturally in cow's milk. When a dog ingests a dairy product like milk, cheese, or ice cream, the lactose doesn't get digested. Since it doesn't get digested, it ferments in the dog's intestine, which causes diarrhea and flatulence (always so much fun).

Some dogs tolerate milk better than do others. If your dog has no problem with a bit of milk, then don't worry about it too much, although milk is not necessary in an adult dog's diet. However, if your dog adores milk but doesn't tolerate it well, try a product that is designed for lactose-intolerant people, one to which lactase has been added to break down the lactose.

dog. The breeder should tell you what kind of schedule the puppy has been on and how to change it as he grows.

Keep the same schedule. Follow your breeder's recommendations for timing of meals. Puppies should not be free-fed, because continual access to food means you'll have greater trouble housetraining. When you feed on a set schedule, your puppy will poop on more of a set schedule. Although nothing is cast in stone when it comes to food going in and coming out, scheduling meals makes a big, positive difference.

The times to feed the puppy pretty much depend on your schedule, when you get up, when you come home. The best approach for puppies under 6 months of age is to feed them at specific times three or four times a day. Puppies between 6 months and 1 year of age can be fed twice a day. Different breeders have personal preferences, so see what they, as well as your veterinarian, suggest. Give your Schnauzer some downtime after each meal, such as a nap or crate time. No playing, romping, walking, and so forth for about an hour or hour and a half after each meal. Playing after a meal can lead to an upset stomach.

Because of their rapid growth, puppies need more water per pound (kg) than adults dogs do, given equivalent weights. The growth process creates a lot of by-products and wastes that gather in the dog's blood. Those wastes must be removed, and water is the mechanism to flush wastes through the kidneys and remove it.

Around 3 to 4 months of age, puppies begin teething, a process during which they lose their baby teeth and their adult teeth come in. Their gums and jaws hurt, and chewing helps alleviate the discomfort. That's why people lose such items as shoes, door moldings, couches, and pillows to teething puppies: The puppies are trying to make themselves feel better. Plus, some teething puppies get a bit picky about eating and may even lose their appetite.

Make Housetraining Easier

To make housetraining easier, schedule when your puppy drinks, but let him drink all he wants when he *is* allowed to drink, so that he gets enough water every day.

Puppies are eager eaters who need to be fed several times a day. Your puppy's breeder can give you insight into your pup's eating habits.

"Most breeders have their own methods of introducing puppies to solid food," says breeder Pat Discher. "We start blending 'gruel' for them at about 3 to 4 weeks. As they start licking it, they get more and more. As their teeth come in, we go to soaking kibble to soften it and then eventually just adding water."

For this, Discher uses small-sized puppy food. At some point, usually around 6 to 8 weeks, she changes them over to unmoistened puppy kibble, and her puppies leave for their new homes on that food.

"I am a member of many of the major food company's breeder

Water: The Essential Nutrient of Life

Fresh water is critical to life and essential to digestion. Water should be available at all times for dogs, with the exception of puppies who are on a food and water schedule for housetraining. Just like humans, dogs can survive longer without food than they can without water. A dog can be starving and survive without almost any body fat and only half of his muscle mass, but a dog who loses 15 percent of his body fluids will die. If the water in your area has a lot of lead, chlorine, or other contaminants, filter it before you give it to the dog, or buy bottled water. Another reason to provide filtered or bottled water is that many diseases are waterborne, such as cryptosporidium, giardia, leptospirosis, and *Escherichia coli*. You can undo the benefit of a good diet by giving water with too many chemicals in it. Tip: Don't use distilled water. Essential minerals, necessary to fluid absorption, have been removed.

programs, and I request puppy packs for all our new families. Some of them give small bags of food in their packets. I also send a bag of what the pup is on with them, but the owner sometimes changes foods, often depending on availability. I recommend a good, quality food though, if they do change.

"While the pups are still here, we feed often in the beginning. By the time they are ready to leave, they are getting three meals a day of about a 1/2 cup each. They will gradually eliminate the last meal of the day themselves by not eating it all. At that point, I recommend that they be fed twice a day," Discher says. "For those pups who stay at our house, we leave them on puppy food until they are almost a year old."

Adults

While you can get away with feeding an adult dog once a day, it's not ideal. It's hard on a body to only eat once daily. Besides, food is so critical to a dog's enjoyment of life that feeding twice a day instead of once doubles the joy. Do you feel well if you only eat once a day, every day? A few people do but most don't—the same is true for dogs.

The body must metabolize an entire day's worth of food at once, which makes the pancreas and other digestive organs work harder. It's a bit like having Thanksgiving dinner every day, with no snacking before or after. You'll have an easier time controlling your Schnauzer's weight when his metabolism runs more evenly.

Adulthood is a time when it is most necessary to adjust the amount of food your dog gets to meet his individual needs. Keep an eye on the scale, and give a little bit more or less as necessary.

Adult dogs need protein, fat, and carbohydrates for energy. Nutritional needs vary for dogs even within a breed because requirements differ depending on activity level, health, stress, and medical conditions. If your dog competes in agility, he will need a bit more protein, fat, and calories than will a dog whose main exercise is going for twice-daily walks around the neighborhood or following you up and down the stairs.

Seasons have an effect on food intake, too. Because cold temperatures may cause greater calorie burn to maintain body heat, dogs may need a bit more food during winter than during a hot, lazy summer. (By winter, I mean the kind of climate where snow is in abundance and it's below freezing for months, not the kind of winter where you feel an occasional need for a sweater and don't go for walks because it's cold outside the house.)

However, winter is a not a license to feed tons of extra food. Just a tad more food is needed, not a lot. Miniature Schnauzers don't need that much food in the first place, so an extra bit does not mean doubling the quantity. Some dogs may need a little more weight in winter to help keep them warm, but for Miniature Schnauzers, that means about a pound (kg) or maybe two (0.9 kg) more than their summer weight.

If your dog is seriously underweight, whether from a medical condition or life on the streets before adoption, talk to your veterinarian about the preferred approach for that dog's nutritional needs.

If your dog is overweight, do something about it now. Stop giving any treats other than vegetables, increase his exercise, and talk to your vet about the amount of food he should get. It's always possible that overweight dogs have a thyroid condition, so if less calories and additional exercise don't take the weight off,

Miniature Schnauzers rarely pass up an opportunity for a meal. Adult dogs should be fed twice a day.

have your veterinarian check your Miniature Schnauzer's thyroid with a simple blood test. The medication for this condition is inexpensive but usually must be given for the rest of the dog's life.

Pregnant or Nursing Bitches

Bitches who are pregnant and who then nurse puppies need a significant amount of extra food. Both pregnancy and nursing consume many additional calories, and nutrition is critical.

A nutritious diet can enhance the best qualities of a purebred Mini Schnauzer.

Breeder Pat Discher begins feeding extra amounts of regular food approximately 4 weeks before whelping should occur. During the last week of pregnancy, Discher switches her pregnant dogs to puppy food; by this time, she is giving the dog up to three times their normal amount of food. During nursing, Discher continues with that same level (three times normal), and she feeds twice a day.

Each breeder has her own approach and preferences, so if your breeder is doing something different, don't worry.

Seniors

As dogs age, they need fewer calories and less protein and fat, but they may need a bit more fiber. Seniors start to lose more of the electrolytes, vitamins, and minerals through their kidneys because they don't absorb them as well as they used to. Some dogs must have their foods changed, and some do very well on just a bit less of their regular maintenance food.

Commercial food formulated for seniors is available, but check with your veterinarian before switching just because your Miniature Schnauzer is 10 years old. Some sources think that once a dog hits the last third of his expected life span, he should move to a senior diet. That is not always necessary, although sometimes it's helpful. It depends on your dog's health.

For older dogs experiencing some degree of renal failure, a diet with a lower percentage of protein may be preferable. Some senior dogs get a little constipated, which is why additional fiber in the diet may help.

You can select a commercial diet that is higher in fiber, or add wheat bran to the regular food. Psyllium husk can help too, but because it's a powder, people often mix it with canned food, which is a bit high in calories for senior dogs (at least for those who have the dental capacity to eat harder food). It can be mixed with the pureed vegetables given in raw diets without adding additional calories.

If your senior Schnauzer loses interest in food, many reasons are possible. One is dental trouble: Pain in the mouth often causes dogs to lose their appetite. Dogs can get abscessed teeth, loose teeth, or most likely, gingivitis. Although rare, even cavities are possible reasons for dental pain. Your veterinarian should peek at your dog's pearly whites any time loss of appetite occurs.

It's up to you to monitor your dog's weight. Small dogs with large appetites tend to gain weight quickly and easily.

Dogs lose jaw pressure with age and can't chew the way they used to. Sometimes switching to a smaller-sized kibble does the trick, or adding water to soften it helps. It may also help to switch to smaller, more frequent meals, similar to a puppy feeding schedule.

Other reasons for loss of appetite in older dogs may be medical in nature and should not be taken lightly. If it's not dental, it could be something significant, so take your dog to the veterinarian if inappetence continues.

Occasionally, as dogs age, they lose interest in food without a medical cause behind it. When people age, they tend to be either skinny or overweight, and for the same reason: Some lose interest in or become occupied with food as they age.

Portion Control

It's impossible to simply say "feed a half cup at each meal for a Miniature Schnauzer." The quantity of kibble given depends on the quality of the kibble; more filler and less meat means that you must give more kibble.

Begin by reading the label and learning the recommended portion size. That recommended size is generic and should be adjusted to your dog's activity level and weight. Activity level often goes hand in hand with age, but not always. Two 15-pound (6.8-kg) Miniature Schnauzers may need different amounts of food to remain the same weight.

The size of the servings also depends on your dog's age. Play around with portion until you discover that your dog is not gaining or losing weight on the quantity eaten.

The same goes for home cooked or raw diets. Quantities indicated are always estimates, so experiment to determine what amount it takes for each dog in the household to not gain or lose weight.

OBESITY: A MINI'S ENEMY

Little dogs with a big appetite for life and food, like Miniature Schnauzers, gain weight easily. They are particularly prone to weight gain when soft-hearted, well-meaning owners buckle under those adorable manipulative eyes and give each dog the caloric equivalent of a daily meal in treats.

Lack of exercise, when combined with the extra treats, creates a big problem. Those little rolls of fat might be adorable when they're just starting out, but they can quickly get out of control and take over your dog's health.

Obesity in dogs means being 10 to 25 percent above the ideal weight. The ideal weight for your Miniature Schnauzer depends on your dog's overall structure, so ask your breeder and/or veterinarian what they think the ideal weight for your dog should be.

Most dog owners don't even realize that their dog is overweight; sadly, some know it but don't do anything about it because it's too much fun to give him treats. Sometimes they shrug it off with excuses. Given the negative consequences on the dog's health and

Sample Feeding Schedule

Puppies under 6 months of age:
three times per day

Puppies over 6 month and under 12 months:
twice a day

Adults:
once or twice daily, but twice is better

Seniors:
continue as possible twice a day, but may need three times a day

the shortening effect obesity has on a dog's life span, it is wise to take a realistic look at your dog's weight and see if something should be changed.

Nestlé Purina Foods conducted a study that proved that dogs who eat comparatively less have longer lives than those who eat more. The study also showed that dogs who eat less and have leaner bodies are healthier and have fewer chronic disease conditions. If you feed to maintain an ideal body condition throughout your dog's life span, you can increase the amount of time you will have to spend with your cherished companion.

Obesity is the largest (no pun intended) nutritional problem among dogs. Estimates of canine obesity range from about 25 to 40 percent of the pet dog population, at least in the United States. However, Nestlé Purina recently came out with a new study indicating that one of every six pets (dogs *and* cats) is overweight. That's a large proportion of American pets, and British pets aren't far behind.

This study also showed that almost half of the pet owners with overweight pets did not recognize that their pets were overweight; 45 percent of owners whose pets were judged in the study as being overweight rated their pet as having an ideal body condition.

The right amount of exercise can help ward off obesity.

Take an honest look at your Miniature Schnauzer; better yet, ask your veterinarian if your dog is at a healthy weight. Once people recognize that their dogs are overweight, they can do something about it.

Is Your Dog Overweight?

A rib check is the fastest way to check if your dog is overweight. Simply put, if you can't feel your dog's ribs, your Miniature Schnauzer is overweight. Of course, it's not quite that simple.

To evaluate a dog's body condition, veterinarians use a scoring system from Purina that has 9 points. A score of 9 is very, very bad, because it means the dog is morbidly obese. A score of 4.5 is just where your dog should be. A score of 1 is typically seen in strays or abandoned pets.

Start out checking your Miniature Schnauzer's body condition by feeling his ribs. You should be able to feel them easily without poking around searching for them—"I know they're in there somewhere!" There should be a tiny bit of fat covering them, for protection, but you should be able to feel each individual rib.

If you can't feel them at all, it's time for a diet and more exercise. If you can see the ribs without even touching the dog, especially from a distance, the dog needs some additional weight. Repeat the process over the dog's body. Again, if you can't feel bones such as the spine, shoulders, or hips, or those near the base of the tail, your dog is really overweight. If a bone sticks out visibly, your dog is underweight. Ribs are the most tell-tale spot, so that's why you start the check there.

Take a peek at your dog from above. An honest peek, that is, not an "I'm going to see what I want to see, no matter what the reality is" peek. Dogs should have a waistline behind their ribs.

If you look at your dog from the side, he should have an abdominal tuck. In other words, the area behind your Miniature Schnauzer's ribs should be smaller than his chest.

Losing Weight

It happens to the best of us, dogs and people, particularly as we age. The pounds add up a bit faster than they used to, and it takes less calories to maintain the same weight. More often, though, it's just a matter of too much fuel and insufficient activity. If your dog is too fat to enjoy a walk, it's past time to do something, but better late than never. Any weight you can take off a pleasantly plump Mini may lengthen his life span.

If your dog must lose weight, start by eliminating or reducing treats and completely eliminating table scraps. Too many treats, even those given with love and adoration, add up the calories fast. Table scraps are a huge source of unnecessary calories. Dogs really don't need pancakes with syrup, although they enjoy them. You can also switch to diet kibble, but in many cases, all your Miniature Schnauzer needs is fewer treats and more exercise.

If your dog is gaining weight, the first thing to do is to get him up and moving.

It might help to substitute toys for treats; your dog will still have fun, and he might burn some calories playing with the toy. Also, consider substituting green beans or carrots. Your dog gets the excitement of getting a treat, but it doesn't have as many calories or fat as most ready-made treats.

The second main action is to increase exercise. This will make your dog happy for several reasons. Miniature Schnauzers are active dogs by nature, but if they've been allowed to become couch potatoes, they will age faster and gain weight sooner. If no medical problems prohibit exercise, get out there with them. They need more walks, more play sessions, and more activity, as well as the socialization that comes with it.

It helps to remember that overweight dogs are at increased risk for such health problems as heart disease, arthritis, pancreatic problems, liver problems, diabetes, and rupture of the anterior cruciate ligament. Fat dogs have shorter, unhealthier, more uncomfortable, and expensive lives than do dogs who maintain an appropriate weight. Sorry to be so blunt, but that's the way it is.

It's surprisingly easier to take weight off an obese dog than to get a sick, underweight dog who's uninterested in food to gain weight. Taking it off is relatively easy because you control what goes in your dog's mouth. Keeping it off is a separate concern. If

When to Feed Additional Calories

Hard exercise in winter temperatures means that your Schnauzer may need a few additional calories, because exercising in cold weather burns more calories than exercising in warm weather; the body works harder to maintain normal temperature. The key here is a few calories. Not an extra meal, not 14 more treats per day, just a bit more food. Dogs who are not getting their usual amount of exercise and are spending large portions of the winter snoozing on the couch do not need the extra calories. Rather, they need less.

your dog hits his perfect weight, finally, and you go back to giving table scraps and too many treats, all that effort will have been for nothing, and your dog's weight will creep right back up again.

Obesity-Related Diseases

Dogs really are like people: Overweight dogs are liable to get diseases that dogs of an appropriate weight don't tend to get. They're not just at risk for these diseases, but prone to them. It's a direct correlation. Overweight dogs are likely to be diagnosed with diabetes mellitus; orthopedic problems such as cruciate ligament ruptures and herniated intervertebral disks; heart disease, including congestive heart failure; respiratory disease; kidney disease; liver disease; potentially life-threatening pancreatitis; mammary tumors; and bladder cancer. They are more likely to have strokes and heart attacks.

Some diseases, such as arthritis, epilepsy, tracheal collapse, and respiratory disease, are further aggravated by weight gain. Obesity can cause difficulties with reproduction and birthing. Surgery takes longer because fatty tissue is highly vascular and likely to bleed more during surgery than is lean tissue, and anesthesia use is more complicated with overweight patients.

Being overweight complicates the use of pharmaceutical drugs and slows down recovery from injuries. Obesity increases exercise and heat intolerance. Obese dogs are more likely to have skin problems than non-obese dogs, and may have weakened immune systems as a result of their weight.

TABLE MANNERS

It is up to you, the alpha owner, to establish good table manners in your Miniature Schnauzer. Dogs should not beg at the table, be given table scraps at the table, paw someone's knee to beg, jump on a kitchen chair to stare at someone while they eat, or bark to notify you that they are starving to death while there is a bite of pot roast you're obviously not using.

If you allow them to get away with this bad behavior, you may well allow them to eat excessive calories—in addition to making a frustrated visitor or family member take a swat at your dog. A dinner guest has every right to be upset if your Schnauzer sticks his tongue in her food or paws her ankles while she's trying to eat. You may think this kind of thing is cute, but—trust me on this—no one else does.

Your dog should eat out of his own bowl at the assigned place where he eats every meal—not from your lap, your hands, the counter, or the top of the dining table.

GROOMING
Your Miniature Schnauzer

The Miniature Schnauzer has hair, not fur, which is why this breed is considered hypoallergenic. The hair does not shed and must be cut. "Non-shedding," however, is a bit of a misnomer, really; non-shedding dogs *do* shed, but only a tiny bit, compared to your basic Labrador Retriever, who sheds every time he breathes.

Grooming is a significant consideration for this breed and should be done every 4 to 6 weeks, even for pets who are not show dogs.

ACCEPTING GROOMING

If a new Schnauzer owner has done her homework, she's gone to a dog show and seen Miniature Schnauzers languidly being groomed like some kind of bearded southern belle who has misplaced her mint julep.

Unfortunately, some new pet owners assume that, because the breed gets so much grooming, grooming behavior genes are encoded into the Schnauzer DNA. They believe that a Mini Schnauzer puppy is born knowing to stand calmly while electric clippers or sharp scissors are whizzing around. That assumption is incorrect.

Each one of those gorgeous, perfectly groomed show dogs started out as a puppy who had to be introduced to grooming equipment over time. Because these dogs were raised from birth to be show dogs, their breeder and owners approached them gently when they were very young and introduced them

A dog likes nothing as much as individual, full attention from his favorite person or from anyone he loves. Grooming, by definition, requires that you pay full attention to one dog.

Snuggling up with your darling Mini and brushing him, trimming his nails, and checking his teeth is a bonding experience. Dogs particularly enjoy having your hands run all over their skin — they are getting loved while you're looking for lumps, skin abnormalities, and "Schnauzer bumps" (hard, scabby lesions often seen along the top of a Mini's back).

Feeling your hands rub him all over makes your dog happy and calm, and this reaction is mutual — running your hands all over your dog makes you happy and calm, too. It's a win-win situation. It lowers blood pressure for you both, makes each of you just a tiny bit fonder of each other, and ensures that it's a better day than you would have otherwise had.

Brushing, touching, brushing teeth, looking for mats in the coat, and checking toenail length all contribute to a dog's sense of well-being and feeling loved. Using an electric clipper means that you have built a solid relationship with your dog. You can look her in the eye as you trim her face and use it as a chance to whisper sweet nothings in her clean little ear.

slowly to grooming equipment.

These dogs didn't start out by having a novice race up with an adult-size guillotine-type toenail clipper and attack each toenail as though it were a sporting competition.

If your dog is a puppy when he arrives in your home, take the time to introduce him slowly to different pieces of equipment. Don't try to use the slicker brush and toenail clipper and comb together in the first few sessions. Have one short session for the slicker brush, and later on another short session for the comb, and so on.

Approach him gently, and praise him when he is good. Don't push your luck by expecting him to tolerate much because he was "so good on the first nine toes." Your dog's reaction to that tenth toe might negatively color his perception about toenail grooming for the rest of his life.

If your dog is an adult when he becomes part of your family, he should already have been introduced to grooming, but that doesn't mean he was, or that it was done properly, or that he likes it. If the dog is new to you, approach him slowly in the same manner as you would a puppy until you know how he reacts to the equipment. He may fall asleep or he may try to bite the clipper. It's possible that whoever groomed your adult dog before you didn't know how to groom properly and may have hurt him so that he now hates grooming. Hard to tell—so it's best to have a slow go at it and not try to do it all in one sitting.

GROOMING TOOLS

Appropriate grooming equipment for any size Schnauzer includes wire slicker brushes, trimming scissors, and comb; clippers are easiest for pets who are not show dogs. Show dogs need such equipment as rakes, coarse and fine stripping shears, flat bristle brush, witch hazel, ear powder, and a grooming stone.

Do you really *need* a grooming table? For a pet, not really. Put a rubber bath mat on the kitchen counter near an electrical outlet for the clipper. However, it is easier to groom a dog when his head is restrained by a neck noose, equipment that is available on a grooming table. If you feel that a grooming table will help you, by all means invest in one.

Show dogs are used to being groomed on an elevated surface.

BRUSHING

The more furnishings your dog has, the more frequently he should be brushed. If the dog is heavily furnished, wears a sweater, or gets wet from rain or snow, brushing him every day will make a difference.

Always brush in the direction of the coat, except on the legs. On the legs, brush the hair up an inch (2.5 cm) at a time and then down. Follow up the brushing with a comb to check your work, and make sure you've got all mats and snarls out. A slicker brush works best for both the wiry topcoat and the soft undercoat. The best choice is a large, universal slicker brunch. A stiff bristle brush can be used on the body and is used most often for dogs whose coats are *stripped* (a method of plucking out dead hair). Choose a coarse-toothed metal comb that has approximately 20 wide teeth and 40 narrow teeth.

BATHING

Brush the coat out thoroughly before putting your dog into the bath. Your Miniature Schnauzer's coat will mat far less that way, and you will have less unpleasant work to do. Place a cotton ball into each ear—don't jam it, just gently insert it—to keep the insides of the ear dry and help prevent ear infections.

Wet the dog down with warm water, not hot, because hot water

When to Bathe

Breeder Karen Brittan of Britmor Schnauzers suggests bathing the Miniature Schnauzer either before stripping or immediately afterward so that the opportunity for a staph infection to start in any broken skin is lessened.

can scald a dog's skin. After you have completely wet the coat, lather in a dog shampoo. It's not going to hurt your dog if you use cat shampoo, but it could hurt your cat to use dog shampoo. In either case, it's preferable not to use people shampoo, because pet shampoos are designed for a dog's different pH balance.

DRYING

Dry your dog either by leaving him alone entirely after toweling him off or using a blow dryer that is made especially for dogs. Be careful to use a dryer that offers cooler settings so that your dog's skin doesn't become irritated. Human hair dryers may run too hot, because human skin can take higher heat than can a dog's.

Using a hair dryer to dry your dog can be a real gift in cooler temperatures, because it keeps your dog from getting chilled. It's important to monitor your dog while he's drying so that he doesn't get too hot. Keep the dryer moving so that you don't burn his skin.

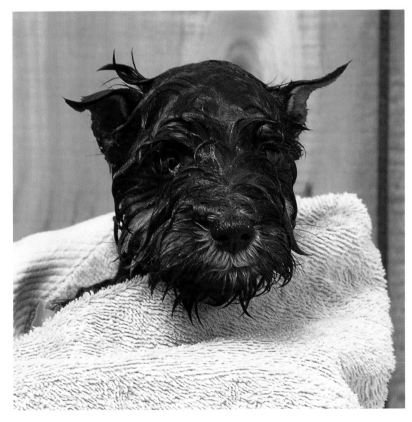

*Your puppy will soon come
to appreciate bath time if
it's not too frequent and it's
done properly.*

CUTTING THE COAT

For Miniature Schnauzers, cutting or trimming the coat is the biggest part of grooming. To keep the cut in the style outlined by the standard takes work and know-how. Show dogs and pets follow exactly the same pattern—the only difference is in how it is achieved.

Beard

Try not to leave too much hair at the outer corner of the eyes. Scissor from the corner of the eye to the corner of the mouth, an area about 1/4 to 1/2 an inch (0.6 to 1.3 cm) long. Blend the cheek in with the beard so that, when you look down on the dog's head, it looks like a brick.

Ears

Keep the hair on the ears short. Always trim with the grain of the hair (the direction in which it grows).

Eyebrows

The eyebrow hair should hang halfway down the muzzle. Comb the eyebrows forward with the metal comb and cut carefully, starting at the outer corner of the eye.

STRIPPING

Show dogs are *stripped* or *rolled*, whereas most pet dogs are clipped. Stripping is used on show dogs to maintain the wiry coat required in the ring. Some pet owners learn to strip, despite the time it takes, so that they can maintain the correct coat color and texture. Stripping pulls out the softer undercoat and dead hairs on a regular basis so that the dog is left with the appropriate wiry overcoat. Stripping encourages the growth of the original color and wiry texture of hair, whereas clipping causes most coats to lighten and soften. Equipment needed to cut and strip the coat includes trimming scissors, clippers, slicker brushes, and stripping knife. Even if you strip, you'll use a clipper on the lighter-colored hair, such as on the rear end, groin area, cheeks, ears, and front.

The pads of the feet are usually clipped. Stripping, or *plucking* as it is sometimes called, can be done using nothing more than two fingers on your own warm little hand. No tools are necessary, although the use of a stripping knife or a contour file is easier.

Grooming as a Health Check

Grooming is not only meant to improve appearance; it's an effective method of preventive health care. While you are grooming him, running your hands over and looking carefully at your dog's entire body allows you to find potentially troublesome lumps, parasites, matted hair that irritates skin, small wounds, runny eyes, and even bad breath. Skin is a significant prognosticator of a dog's health and nutrition, so check it too.

The sooner you find problems, the better your dog will be. Most lumps turn out to be benign and problem free, but for those that are not, it's best to know as soon as possible. Getting parasites, such as fleas, under control and removing ticks can make a huge difference in your dog's health. When the Miniature Schnauzer is groomed regularly, the shorter coat makes many potential problems much easier to see.

Did You Know?

Schnauzers lose most of their coat while undergoing chemotherapy, just as people do.

However, clipping is significantly faster and cheaper. Many professional groomers do not know how to strip because it is too time consuming, and most pet owners won't pay for it.

To *roll* means to remove dead hairs from the overcoat using your finger and thumb. This encourages the new coat to grow continuously. (It is also called *plucking*, which is really a more accurate description.) The physical action is simple—just pluck—but it takes ongoing grooming sessions over many months, and the coat is constantly being adjusted. Assign a day to roll the coat, such as every Monday, and you can do this for the lifetime of your dog—he will always look his best.

Stage stripping removes the old coat in a pattern, so that the coat appears to be the same length over the whole body except for the neck and head. Eventually, the whole coat will be too long, and you'll have to start all over again.

How to Strip

According to breeder Karen Brittan of Britmor Schnauzers, stripping is simple. It is time-consuming but something that you can do easily when you have spare time. You don't need to go to grooming school to learn how to strip, although it is best to have a knowledgeable person get you started.

Brittan starts by rubbing in some ear powder or white chalk block on the fur

This Miniature Schnauzer has been groomed to perfection for his performance at the Westminster Kennel Club show in New York.

she's going to strip. She uses one hand to stretch out the skin of the chosen patch and plucks with the other. She suggests that you might also try gently pinching the skin between your thumb and index finger while pulling with the other hand.

Sometimes she also uses a contour file or a stripping knife. A contour file is similar to the pumice stone you may use on your own feet.

"There are two very important things to remember: Keep your wrist rigid, and don't pull the hair out with a twisting motion. That twisting motion causes the hair to be cut when your goal is to pull it out," says Brittan.

The proper technique is more important for your hand and wrist than it is for the dog. Stripping requires a lot of repetitive motion, and if you are not careful, it can cause pain and inflammation in your wrist. She recommends that you pull from the shoulder, while keeping your arm fairly immobile.

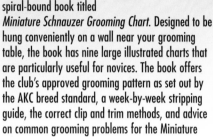

Grooming Chart

The American Miniature Schnauzer Club sells a spiral-bound book titled *Miniature Schnauzer Grooming Chart*. Designed to be hung conveniently on a wall near your grooming table, the book has nine large illustrated charts that are particularly useful for novices. The book offers the club's approved grooming pattern as set out by the AKC breed standard, a week-by-week stripping guide, the correct clip and trim methods, and advice on common grooming problems for the Miniature Schnauzer.

Done correctly, stripping is not painful to the dog, although it can irritate the skin. If irritation occurs, a medicated shampoo can alleviate it.

"Always, always keep the [dog's] skin taut, because the hair comes out easier," said Brittan. She also says to pull the hair in the direction in which it is growing, otherwise it will be painful.

Pulled out in the correct direction and manner, stripping is a simple, non-irritating procedure, because you're pulling out dead hair. To your dog, it feels somewhat similar to you having your hair brushed deeply and thoroughly—you don't feel the individual hairs coming out on your brush because they're dead. Most dogs don't have a problem with having it done.

Section by Section

Brittan recommends stripping in sections because the Miniature Schnauzer's coat grows faster on some parts of the body than it does others. The hair grows the most quickly on the dog's head and front, so those are the last areas to be stripped before a show. The goal here is to have a dog with a full, even coat with no dead hair by show time. Typically, show people begin stripping their Miniature Schnauzers approximately 10 weeks prior to a dog show.

The process is broken down into several stages, although some people break it down into even smaller stages, depending on the dog's individual structure. The first stage is the largest area, and it

Rolling is a technique used by professional Schnauzer groomers in which the longest hairs on the dog's coat are "rolled" out on a regular basis.

consists of the area down the back of the neck, widening to behind the shoulder blades, running down the rib cages to behind the elbows, up a diagonal to the front of the rear leg, and down the thighs.

The second stage, done the following week, covers the sides of the neck, the tail, and the rest of the shoulders. The third and last stage includes the head, face, and front of the dog.

Brittan says that several patterns of stripping can be used. Find one that makes sense to you, because no technique is any better or worse than another, as long as the finished coat looks the way you want it to. She is quick to point out that stripping has many benefits: A stripped coat is harder, repels dirt and water, and doesn't mat as easily as a clipped coat.

Strip by Color

Interestingly enough, dogs who have salt-and-pepper coats and those with black-and-silver coats have all the darker parts of their coat stripped but not the lighter areas. Brittan says that the creamy white areas are untouched by stripping and are usually clipped with a #10 blade. On solid black dogs, the entire coat is stripped.

Brittan lightly strips the head, front, and sides of the neck; the hair in these areas grows quickly.

She also rakes the coat every week to keep the undercoat from overwhelming the top coat. The undercoat grows constantly. To rake, pull a stripping knife through the coat to catch the undercoat; as with stripping, keep the skin taut. Once the coat comes in, do this once a week.

Rolling

Rolling a coat is similar to stripping and mostly differs in the timing of when the hair is pulled. In stripping, the hair in each section you've stripped is the same length and age. It grows out and blows (dies), and in a few weeks you need to strip again. A rolled coat has strands of hair in layers of different lengths and ages. With rolling, you pull the longest hairs all over the dog on a weekly basis, all year round, so that the whole coat always looks neat and ready for a show.

Brittan feels it is easiest to start rolling a coat on a longer-coated dog. If you start rolling a recently stripped dog, you must decide which hairs to pull, as opposed to simply pulling the longest hairs. According to Brittan, rolling can be described as plucking about every twelfth hair in the coat once a week.

After you begin rolling and before you're finished, the coat looks pretty terrible in a nasty moth-eaten way. It takes several months to get a coat properly rolled and in good shape; good results probably won't appear before 3 months, and it may take longer.

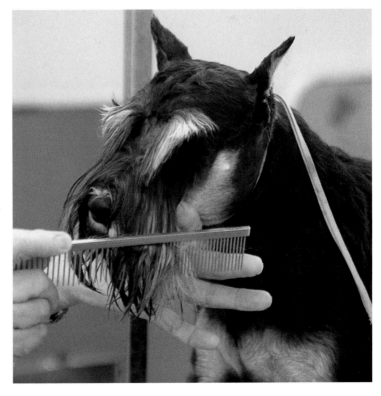

The beard is one of the Mini Schnauzer's most distinctive features. This dog is being readied for his time in the show ring.

If you have not been rolling a dog since puppyhood, then timing when to begin rolling is critical for show dogs, because the coat must be at an appropriate stage for the ring. Always remember that the hair you pull today will be the show coat in 8 to 10 weeks. It takes 4 weeks for that hard coat to break through the skin.

"The best rolled coats are those with a good harsh texture, a minimum of undercoat, with a tendency for the coat to come in fairly rapidly," says Brittan. "If your dog

Experienced Mini Schnauzer groomers know they need to keep a picture in their heads of what the whole dog will look like when he's fully groomed so that they can do each part of the job correctly.

has a lot of undercoat or the coat is too soft, you are better off stage stripping it."

She recommends that you begin rolling puppies when they are around 8 to 12 weeks. Use a grooming stone or coarse stripping knife, and begin raking through the coat in the correct pattern.

The body is the easiest area to roll, but it becomes more difficult on other parts—head, sides of neck, front—because one must actually pull a bit of live coat each week in those areas to maintain the coat at the correct length. Brittan pulls systematically in rows, but warns that staying in one spot too long creates holes.

Brittan has two rules about rolling:

1. Never, ever cut the coat with shears of any kind, not even with thinning shears, under any circumstances. Cutting completely defeats the purpose of rolling.
2. You must faithfully work the coat at least once a week; otherwise, it will take weeks to get the coat rolling properly again.

Where to Begin

Because there is no established, "correct" method for rolling, most people have their own system. Brittan begins by raking over the whole coat, first with the coarse stripping knife, then the fine one (you are raking, not cutting), to pull out some of the undercoat and any dead outer coat. Her second step is to go through the longer parts with her fingers and remove the longest hairs.

She starts at one point, usually around the withers, and then radiates out. Then she moves to the shorter areas of the coat that she has pulled with stripping knives. "I never pull more than two times in the same area. However, if the coat is now rolling correctly, the blades will only pull out the necessary hair and leave the proper length of hair untouched under the blade," said Brittan.

Next, she uses the grooming stone over the whole dog to remove any longer hairs that might have been missed. After that, she combs through the coat to look for bumps in the coat that indicate longer hairs that were missed.

Brittan prefers rolling to stripping, despite the truly significant investment of time. "In the end, the payback is much greater because you will have a dog who can go anywhere at the drop of a hat and *always* look great. Never again will you be plagued by the 'my dog will be out-of-coat by then' syndrome."

CLIPPING

Clipping your Schnauzer's coat doesn't mean your dog will *look* different from the cut portrayed by the breed standard—a look that is achieved by stripping. But he will *feel* different. The difference is in the texture of the coat, not in its style. A coat trimmed with a clipper should end up looking exactly like the formal Miniature Schnauzer cut.

This is not to say that pet dogs must have a show cut. If you prefer a less formal style, by all means, go for it. The point is that if you want the style called for in the standard, you can achieve it with a clipper, and far faster and more conveniently than by stripping. Stripping is usually only done for show dogs because of the amount of time involved.

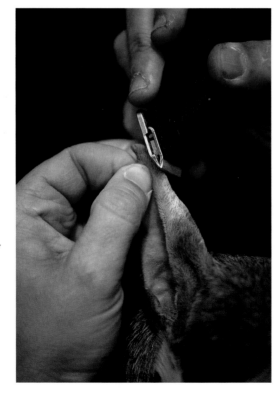

Ears need to be clipped delicately to prevent accidental cutting.

Choosing a Clipper

While everyone understands the allure of saving money, don't buy a low-end clipper. Avoid those that say they are for home use, because they tend to fall apart pretty rapidly—cheap clippers can break after just a few uses. Get a nice mid-range set, where the labeling indicates the product is aimed for the show dog market. You'll save time and money by buying a good one right off the bat, and it will handle better.

Clippers are available both corded and cordless. The corded ones have a bit more power, and you don't run the risk of needing a charge before you're done. A cordless has benefits, particularly for the beginner, in that you don't have to worry about where the cord is or worry about it getting wrapped around the dog's legs.

How to Clip

Before clipping, brush the coat. When ready to trim, a #10 blade should be used for the body and head.

You don't have to do anything in a specific order, so work in whatever order seems natural to you. The following order is a good way to begin.

Start clipping at the base of neck, on the back, and move toward the base of the tail. Clip the body down to a parallel line that's above the elbows of the front legs. The hind legs are to be clipped diagonally from the flank (top of the thigh) to just above the hocks (ankle), while leaving a fringe along the front part of the leg. It helps to fold the leg fringe in toward the inner thigh. Then clip off the hair on the outer thigh in a downward direction, all the way down to the just above the hock.

Next, move to the front of the dog, and clip the neck and chest, starting at where the neck meets the head. Go down to just above the elbow.

For the tail, clip in the direction of hair growth. The area underneath the tail can be clipped against the growth using a #10 blade, or with the growth using a #15 blade (the higher the number, the closer the shave). Be careful around the anus, because the clipper may hurt that sensitive area, and your dog

Should You Learn to Use a Clipper?

For pet Miniature Schnauzers who will not compete in the show ring, using an electric clipper to cut the coat is definitely the way to go. You can either have a professional do it or learn to do it yourself.

If you decide to learn, understand that, in the beginning, your dog will not look like she does when she comes home from the professional groomer. It doesn't matter how often you played hairdresser as a kid or if you clip your spouse's hair. (For one thing, your spouse's head doesn't have joints, and dog legs have a couple of joints that are harder to trim than the body.)

My first attempt at using a clipper resulted in a friend asking if I'd clipped the dog in a food processor. Now I do it on a regular basis, but I still take the dogs to their groomer once a year to get a more professional job and to get the coat back into proportion. In my household, grooming is done either by The Real Groomer or The Genuine Imitation Mommy Groomer. But it's not hard to learn how to clip your Schnauzer, and the hair grows back if you make a mistake.

You develop good bonding with your dog and save a lot of money, time, and hassle by not having to go to a professional. But understand that your dog is not going to have a perfect cut the first few times you use a clipper.

Books and videos are available so that you can see how the process is done. (Videos are often more useful than books when you're first beginning.) You will learn to go with the grain of the coat, how to hold the clipper, what size blade to use, and where to oil the clipper and how often.

What can only be learned by experience is how much pressure it takes to remove hair; a heavy hand will cut the coat too short, and a light hand won't make enough difference. It takes practice and willingness, and the benefits are well worth the effort.

could end up with a grudge against any kind of grooming.

On the head, start by identifying a baseline—such as the eyebrows and corners of the mouth—to use as a point from which to start clipping. Work outward from that baseline. Use parallel horizontal strokes following the direction of hair growth, going from the top of the head down toward the neck. The hair on the muzzle is parted but never clipped or scissored.

Place one hand under the ear and hold it while clipping with the other hand, so that you have something to push against with the clipper. Clip outward from the center of the ears, then finish by scissoring the ear edges. Clipping should be done very carefully on the ears, because a slip could cut the ear and cause a lot of bleeding. (Head wounds are notoriously heavy bleeders.) If that does happen, apply pressure and styptic powder.

The groin can become matted, so clip those hairs off. Help the dog to stand on his back feet while holding up the front of his body under his armpits, or hold the dog by his knees and clip from the naval to just in front of the genitals.

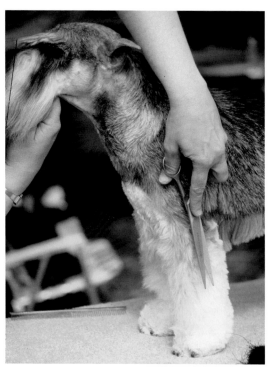

Groomers use scissors to get rid of any fuzzy hairs that may be sticking out; they also use them to shape features like eyebrows.

SCISSORING

After either clipping or stripping, move on to scissoring.

For the feet and legs, use scissors. Trim the hair between the toes and the large foot pad. The goal for the front legs is to have a straight, even balance, so that the hair is circular and resembles a pole. However, keep a line coming down the sides from the shoulder blade to the base of the foot.

Approach the rear legs in basically the same way, but angle and trim the rear arch to give the appearance of a wide-moving rear. Use thinning shears to blend hair on the outer thigh with the leg fringe, so that the outside of the rear leg has a straight line from the thigh to the foot.

Remember to scissor along the outside edge of each ear and get rid of the fuzzy hairs. The muzzle and beard are not trimmed, but the long, parted eyebrows must be shaped. They are a critical component of the Miniature Schnauzer's look. Also, carefully scissor the hair between the eyes, then comb the eyebrows forward, and cut the hair into an inverted V shape. Start at the highest part of the eyebrow and trim at a 45-degree angle.

NAIL TRIMMING

Dogs often view nail trimming as torture. The sooner you teach a puppy to accept nail trimming, the easier time you or a groomer will have with that dog for the rest of his life. Since Miniature Schnauzers have a life expectancy of 12 to 14 years, that's a lot of toenail angst.

Use a sharp trimmer. The blades dull over time. Sharper blades make the whole process easier and more comfortable, not to mention quicker.

The *quick* is that point in the nail where the dog's circulation extends into the nail bed; if you cut past the quick, the nail bleeds. The idea is to cut above the quick, just trimming dead nail. The quick can be tough to see on a Miniature Schnauzer because some or all of the nails are black.

Don't beat yourself up if you do cut into the quick; it happens to everyone once in a while. When you do cut the quick, your dog will let you know about it immediately and in no uncertain terms. (My Miniature Schnauzer would pathetically hold up the bleeding toe and put on an opera-worthy performance of *Sturm und Drang*.)

Just take a clean cloth, paper towel, or tissue, place it over the end of the nail, and apply pressure for 5 to 10 minutes until the bleeding stops. Use a styptic powder or gel to stop the bleeding. The good news is that the more you trim the nails, the more the quick recedes, and the less likely you are to cut it.

EAR CARE

The hair growing inside the ear is supposed to be taken out; otherwise, it can contribute to ear infections and be annoying to the dog. Yeast and bacteria grow wonderfully in deep, moist, dark places like ears. Your dog's ear is a perfect place for infections to start (although Miniature Schnauzers are not terribly predisposed to them, unlike breeds with long, floppy ears such as English Setters or Basset Hounds).

To remove hair from inside the ear, sprinkle some ear powder into the hair-covered areas. The powder helps you grasp the ear hairs with your thumb and finger and pluck the hair out. Only pluck a few hairs simultaneously, because grabbing too many at once could be painful.

Make sure to spread the ear open so that you can see all the hair. We're talking about the visible hairs near the opening of the ear here, not something way down deep. For those deeper hairs, use a hemostat (similar to a pair of scissors but designed for pulling rather than cutting) or a scissors-type tweezer to pluck.

After all this plucking, remove the powder or it will clog the ear. Gently blow on the dog's ear to get him to

If you work carefully and quickly around your dog's nails, trimming just the tips, your Schnauzer will learn that the procedure is painless and fairly fast.

shake out the excess powder. You can also clean it out with a liquid ear cleaner, using a cotton ball or—if you're very gentle—a cotton swab. Be sure to remove dirt and all the powder or cleaner when you're finished.

Ear Infections

Ear infections can range from a minor infection that can be cleared up with antibiotic ointments and flushes to more severe inner or middle ear infections that can have neurological signs, such as permanently paralyzing the side of the face or causing deafness.

Some dogs get chronic ear infections that go away for a while but eventually return, and both the dog and owner feel as though the dog is spending half his life with an ear infection. Few things in veterinary medicine are as frustrating as chronic ear infections. Although Miniature Schnauzers with uncropped ears have pretty good air circulation in their ears, Miniature Schnauzers with cropped ears are a bit less likely to have ear infections than those without cropped ears. The additional exposure to air flow dries out the ears. This doesn't mean that dogs with cropped ears don't get ear infections, though. A healthy ear with no problems is a nice pink color on the inside; a small amount of wax is normal. Problems with an unhealthy ear can be detected by a bad odor from inside the ear(s), swelling, tenderness that causes your dog to react to touch, a large quantity of wax, red skin inside the ear flap, pawing at the head, and shaking the head. Yeast or bacterial infections are treated with ointments, some of which are available by prescription. The ointments are quite messy but effective. Many dogs react to the ointment and what it does by rubbing their ears on the floor, the couch, or on you. The ointment washes out quite well, thankfully.

Left untreated, ear infections get worse. Prevention is valuable if your dog begins to have problems with ear infections. You can regularly flush out your dog's ears using commercial preparations you find at the vet clinic. These flushes help keep the ears dry and clean. Squeeze a few drops of liquid into the ear canal and then gently massage the outside of the ear canal to make sure the flush goes in.

Foreign bodies, such as grass or weed seeds encountered while romping through a field, can get stuck in the ear and cause an

Grooming Clothes

A grooming coat or apron is a wonderful tool to help keep you fur-free while you groom your Schnauzer. You can purchase a coat or apron for yourself at dog shows and pet supply places. These garments are made of a shiny fabric to which dog hair doesn't stick. An astonishing quantity of hair flies around after being clipped. The hair can get in your mouth and stick to your neck, and it can stay on your clothes for approximately half of eternity.

infection. These can become painful enough that your dog will not allow the veterinarian to examine the ear without anesthesia (which can also happen with yeast or bacterial infections). The veterinarian will remove the foreign body with a long forceps and prescribe medication.

Mites can be a problem for any breed. They cause a telltale brown waxy discharge, and as with a yeast ear infection, the dog paws at his ears and shakes his head. Since they are microscopic, you won't be able to see the mites with the naked eye, but your veterinarian can see them using an otoscope. The ears must be flushed and treated.

The Dangers of Cotton Swabs

Cotton swabs can harm a dog's L-shaped ear canal, just as they can harm a human's straight ear canal. Avoid sticking cotton swabs into ears. Swabs can also jam wax farther into the ear, causing additional harm.

EYE CARE

Miniature Schnauzers are fairly prone to "eye gunk," which is a technical term for that bit of mucus that forms in the inside corner of each eye. Use a tissue or cotton ball to remove it.

Excessive discharge is not normal and should be checked by a veterinarian. The inner eyelids should not be swollen or have a yellow discharge.

Hair that hangs into a Schnauzer's eyes can cause irritation. It can also scratch the surface of the cornea, which is very uncomfortable. Take care to avoid letting hair contact the eye.

Grooming is a good time to examine your dog's eyes, which you can do in addition to the suggested annual eye testing. Miniature Schnauzers are prone to hereditary and congenital cataracts and generalized progressive retinal atrophy (PRA). Both of these conditions can lead to blindness, so it's a good idea to look deeply into your dog's small and deep-set oval eyes.

DENTAL CARE

"Eewww, dog breath!" is a nearly universal statement of displeasure triggered by that offensive odor. Given that Miniature Schnauzers are so affectionate and always by your side or in your lap, it's a good idea to stay on top of bad breath for your sake as well as theirs.

Bad breath, or halitosis, is the first sign of periodontal disease. Loose and abscessed teeth are both common and painful. First and foremost in the battle against bad breath is brushing the dog's teeth with a pet toothbrush and pet toothpaste. Human toothpaste should never be swallowed by anyone—human or dog—because of the fluoride and detergents in it. And since dogs are not big on spitting, it's important to use toothpaste designed to be safe to swallow. Rinsing is not needed with pet toothpastes.

Pet toothpastes come in flavors such as poultry, liver, and peanut butter designed to appeal to dogs (most of them aren't big fans of mint). Also, pet-specific toothpastes generally contain enzymes that can help get rid of dental plaque.

Have your vet show you how to brush your dog's teeth properly. Several websites and videos demonstrate the proper method of brushing. Many dental chews and wipes are available at any pet supply store. These should be used in conjunction with brushing, not as a substitute for brushing and regular dental care. Some chews double as treats, but unlike ordinary treats, are designed specifically to improve breath and remove tartar. Wipes are small pieces of moist, treated cloth that you wipe over the dog's teeth to remove tartar. Bottles of dental rinses are available too, as is a gel that can be applied weekly instead of brushing.

Keeping the area around your Mini Schnauzer's eyes clean is good for his health.

How to Brush the Teeth

Veterinarians suggest that a dog's teeth be brushed daily.

Start the process by comforting your dog and holding him while letting him taste a bit of the toothpaste from the tip of your finger. Put a small amount of toothpaste on the brush, and lift his lips.

Begin to slowly brush the front teeth in an up and down motion, just as you do for your own teeth. You don't need to brush the inside surface of the teeth (the side facing the dog's throat) because tartar usually doesn't build up there.

Make sure to brush the line where the gum and teeth touch.

Brush each side of the mouth for approximately 30 seconds. Brush slowly and gently. Be certain you get the back teeth, because most problems are more likely to turn up there.

Because pet toothpaste is swallowed, it doesn't matter if any of it sticks in your Miniature Schnauzer's beard or moustache to be licked off later.

If you begin brushing a puppy's teeth when you get him, the process won't be a problem. Most dogs who have real issues about toothbrushing didn't get brushed when they were puppies. If you get a rescue or a stray, you might not have any information about a brushing history; start slowly, as though the dog were a puppy.

Some dogs fight brushing (and for some dogs, that's an understatement). If you give up and walk away because they're fussing, then it's only going to be a more difficult task next time around. Stick to your plan and finish the procedure while talking to your dog softly and sweetly. Use the tasty flavored toothpaste as its own reward.

Some dogs may never calmly accept brushing no matter what you do. If this is the case, do the best you can with dental chews, wipes, rinses, hard biscuits, and commercial food designed to prevent plaque and tartar buildup. These products do not replace toothbrushing, and are normally viewed as an extra tool, but if that's all the dog will accept, they are more beneficial than no cleaning at all. It is far, far better to teach your dog to accept toothbrushing.

Deeper Cleaning

Most dogs should have an annual dental cleaning, done under anesthesia and performed by a veterinarian. Anesthesia is significantly safer and better today than it was several years ago, when many people delayed dental cleanings because they didn't want their pet to have unnecessary anesthesia. However, the health risks from periodontal disease are now more significant than risk from anesthesia.

The anesthesia serves several purposes. Most important, it keeps the dog still so that the veterinarian can clean beneath the gum line (called the subgingival area), because this task is difficult indeed if the dog is conscious. It also provides pain control, so that the dog is comfortable during such procedures as removing calculus and tooth polishing.

Also, during anesthesia, a breathing tube is placed into the dog's windpipe—one benefit of that tubing is that the bacteria-covered plaque scaled off the teeth doesn't go into the dog's respiratory system, which could result in an infection in the heart or other organs.

Dogs who have significant problems with their teeth should have professional cleanings done on an as-needed basis. Thankfully, unlike toy breeds, Miniature Schnauzers do not have a breed-specific propensity for dental problems because they have enough room in their mouths for all their teeth.

Dental Disease

Periodontal disease is caused by plaque, which is 80 percent bacteria and 20 percent food and saliva. You must remove plaque every single day because, if it is not removed, it mineralizes and

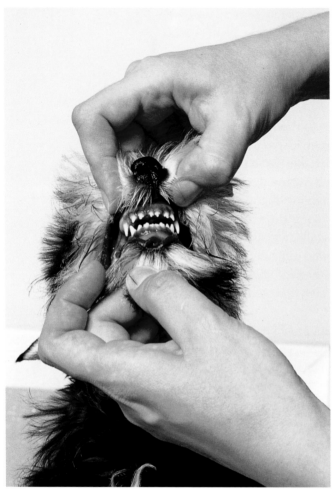

If you want your dog's teeth to stay healthy and his breath to remain fresh, you will need to brush them regularly. Your veterinarian can show you how.

forms tartar. Tartar is bad—it can lead to a bacterial infection in the mouth.

Unfortunately, this infection most likely won't just stay in the mouth. It can enter the bloodstream and spread to other organs, such as the kidneys, liver, and heart. This potential spread of bacteria is the reason dental care is so critical to your dog's overall health.

Additionally, periodontal disease is painful to dogs, although they often show no sign of discomfort other than perhaps pawing at their mouths. Chronic pain can alter behavior and temperament, so if you see these signs, check your dog's teeth and gums.

Sadly, pet owner compliance is lower for toothbrushing than for any other pet care task. (My vet's clinic estimates that only 5 percent of dog owners brush their dog's teeth regularly.) A few years ago, people thought they didn't have to brush their dog's teeth and pretty much laughed at such a notion. Now they know it is necessary, but like going to the gym, most people don't do it as often as they know they should.

Bad breath can be more than a mere nuisance: It can be an indicator of some fairly serious diseases. There's bad dog breath, and there's really, really bad, stomach-turning breath that occurs even though your dog hasn't snuck into the cat's litter box. If you take good care of your dog's teeth, and his breath is still noticeably bad, it's time to go to the vet to see if a medical cause, such as diabetes mellitus or kidney disease, is present.

Learning to groom your Miniature Schnauzer is something that anyone in the family can enjoy.

TRAINING and BEHAVIOR
of Your Miniature Schnauzer

No matter what activities—if any—you decide to train for, the first goal all dog owners should have is to train their dog to be a good, livable companion. No one likes a misbehaving dog; no one wants to live with an out-of-control dog.

Your visitors don't want to feel as though they've been mauled at the knees by furiously barking Miniature Schnauzers when they enter your house. Only you can decide if you mind living with a dog who barks furiously when the mail is delivered, a dog who won't sit or stay, or who won't come when called.

Do you care if your dog pulls you all over the sidewalk on a walk? The more you care about your dog behaving politely, the more willing you will be to train your dog.

THE IMPORTANCE OF POSITIVE TRAINING

Years ago, training dogs consisted mostly of yelling "no!" and whapping them with rolled-up newspapers. Using that approach, it's surprising that any adult dog ended up with a nice temperament. Miniature Schnauzers thrive on positive training, in which you praise and treat them repeatedly for correct behavior and don't yell when they don't get it. Corrections are given with a positive "you'll get it next time" attitude.

Clicker training is a prime example of positive training; it is often called *operant conditioning*. It reinforces correct responses, which are praised repeatedly. The noise from the clicker lets your Mini know *immediately* that he's performed the requested behavior correctly, which results in getting praise and a treat. For the behavior that isn't quite what you asked for, there is no noise from the clicker. Your Mini will associate the clicker noise with "I got it right!"

Why Punishment Doesn't Work

Dogs will be dogs. Particularly before they are mature and well trained, you will most likely find some dog behavior frustrating. Digging, barking, mouthing, not coming when called—all this may be unacceptable to you.

Punishing a Miniature Schnauzer for problem behaviors doesn't work. Miniature Schnauzers don't respond well to negative input; it simply increases stress and anxiety. Because stress is often the root of a problem behavior, the punishment makes the problem worse rather than corrects it.

If your dog chews because she's nervous about your being gone, screaming at her for chewing after the fact is only going to make her seek more stress relief, which is likely to be more chewing. It's a cycle with no end. Dogs sometimes repeat the unwanted behavior to get your attention because, to dogs, the bad attention of punishment is better than no attention. In frustration, some people resort to punishing the dog. Punishment includes hitting the dog with your hand or an object like a newspaper, yelling, pushing,

Flunking Obedience

Many dogs must take a remedial beginning obedience class. This is not a formal offering at dog school; it's just a repeat of beginning obedience. It's not like being held back a grade if your dog doesn't go directly from beginning to intermediate obedience; his peers will not shun him, and he's not going to feel like the stupid kid at the bottom of the class. He will not know the difference.

If you get to the end of your first obedience class and your Schnauzer has only reliably mastered half of it, you're both going to find the subsequent class frustrating and unsuccessful because the work builds directly on what is learned in the first class. Wait to take the intermediate class when you're both ready—when your dog has shown that he listens to your commands and that he can do reliably what is required in beginning obedience.

Many obedience instructors put their dogs through the first beginning obedience class several times to reinforce it, because everything that is fun later on, such as agility, rally, flyball, and freestyle, needs the solid foundation of basic obedience.

throwing things at the dog, rubbing his nose in urine and feces to "teach the dog not to do it," and so on. This is unacceptable behavior from you because you have not taught your Miniature Schnauzer the correct behavior—you have simply taught him to be afraid of you.

If you smack him with a rolled-up newspaper, a legendary but ineffective tool in housetraining from your grandparents' day, you've taught him to be afraid of the newspaper and your hands. There is no canine behavioral equivalent to hitting, and dogs do not understand what it means, other than it's a bad thing. They don't understand it to mean "don't do that."

Remember that a dog's bad behavior usually stems from lack of maturity and training; time will bring maturity, and training is your responsibility.

TRAIN FOR A GOOD COMPANION

Dogs who are out of control are typically the result of an owner's unwillingness to train or a belief that they can't control the dog. Miniature Schnauzers are so smart that they will train you if you don't train them.

Let's re-emphasize that one aspect of Miniature Schnauzers: They are smart. They are really smart. They are smart enough to solve problems and figure out how to get what they want. And what they often want is to see how much they can get away with. If you let them take the upper hand, the battle for a well-behaved dog is pretty much lost.

You train your dogs every single day you live with them, whether you realize it or not. They pick up signals you don't even know you're sending. For example, when my dogs hear the last click of the last leash to be attached to collars, they get very excited because they know that they're going out to have some fun. I did not train them to recognize that the click made from snapping a leash on means anything, but they picked it up on their own. Be aware of what you teach them, unintentionally or otherwise.

The important thing to remember when your adorable puppy walks in your door for the first time is that obedience is not encoded in his DNA. Wanting to please you is certainly part of a Miniature Schnauzer's genetic makeup, and their intelligence makes training significantly easier than it is with some other

Regardless of whether you want to go on to compete in formal obedience with your dog, you should at least train him to understand the basics.

breeds. Still, they are not born knowing what they should do, such as pee outside instead of in the corner of the living room. Formal training is one thing, but having your dog become a good companion is another. One way to do this is through programs like the AKC's Canine Good Citizen program and the Kennel Club's Good Citizen Dog Scheme (see Chapter 7), where the goal is to demonstrate that a dog is well-behaved in public. Each program provides a similar, solid basis for future training and obedience. Even if you never go further than that, you'll have a well-behaved companion who is a joy to have around and who is welcomed by other people. Good canine manners go far in this world and have a lot to do with how often your friends drop by or whether they cringe if you ask to bring your dog with you when you go visit them for coffee and a chat.

Formal obedience is quite different from household manners. After basic obedience training is complete, decide whether you want to go beyond having a livable companion. That doesn't necessarily mean wanting to compete in formal obedience competition, although that's an option. It means thinking about how many classes you might want to take beyond basic obedience, how many books you care to read on the subject, and essentially deciding how you want your Miniature Schnauzer to behave during his 12- to 14-year lifetime in your home.

FINDING THE DOG SCHOOL FOR YOU

Whatever your goal is—good companion or canine competitor—an appropriate training school probably is available for you and your dog. Call your local shelter for a recommendation. Talk to other dog owners. Ask what they liked—and especially what they didn't like—about the training center or the instructor.

Maybe they didn't like it because they had a new instructor who didn't know how to work with people yet. Maybe they didn't like it because the classes weren't well organized. Maybe they didn't like it because they have unrealistic expectations and think that simply showing up for obedience school without practicing at home is training. (It's not; you and your dog doing homework is the most vital component of training.)

It's also a good idea to ask the available training schools if you can attend a session without your dog, to see how the classes work and if you like them.

If you are gearing toward formal obedience competition, look for someone who teaches that specific skill. One sure source for that information is your local kennel club, but other options exist.

BASIC OBEDIENCE

Basic obedience covers a range of behaviors that makes life easier for you. One of the basic tenets of living with a dog is that you are alpha—the provider of resources, food, and affection, and the giver of walks. To maintain that position, require your dog to respond to a basic command, such as Sit or Stay, before he gets dinner or a favorite toy. This guideline isn't just for puppyhood but for his lifetime. There is no reason why an older Schnauzer still should not have to acknowledge that you are in charge.

Each command during training should be preceded with the dog's name, not the other way around. Say "Otto, sit," not "Sit, Otto."

The following brief descriptions of the basic training commands are not meant to imply that you should be able to

You can't train your dog if you don't have his attention. The best way to get his attention is to entice him with something special, like a favorite toy or tasty treat.

train your dog to respond to a command after just a couple of tries (although Schnauzers are so smart, many of them do learn that quickly). Your best bet by far is to take obedience classes and practice daily at home. Results will not be immediate: Training takes patience and repetition. But the payoff in bonding and a well-mannered dog is worth every moment you've invested.

Attention

The world is full of distractions, and puppies are quite easily distracted. For the most effective training, teach your dog to pay attention to you. You are the holder of resources, giver of treats, provider of kisses and dinner. Make sure your dog pays attention to the one who is important here—you.

Have treats with you, but don't let your dog see them. The use of tasty morsels is wonderfully helpful in training, whether it's basic skills now or advanced maneuvers later.

To start, say his name, "Otto!" and then quickly step away from him. When he moves, praise him with your voice and give him a treat. His name is the key word to which he will learn to pay attention to you when you say it.

There are five steps here: Say his name, step away, praise, bring treat out sight-unseen, offer the treat. When you do give your dog the treat, hold it up between your face and his so that your dog makes eye contact with you. (Later, when he gives you eye contact just for the heck of it, treat him for it.) Some people spit food at the dog out of their own mouth so that the dog learns to focus on their owner's face.

Practice getting your dog's attention in sets of about five, and repeat the sets frequently. Do it in places with differing distractions, such as the living room when it's empty, the dog park, waiting for dog class to begin, or sitting in the aisle of the pet supply store when people are walking by and saying "Oh my gosh, what a cute Miniature Schnauzer!"

In this way, your dog learns to focus on you as his leader.

Sit

Sit is the easiest behavior to teach because you can use the dog's natural inclination to move into this position. Hold a treat at your dog's nose level. As his head and neck move forward to take the treat, pull your hand up and right over his head while you say

Body Language and Communication

Typically, dogs show more than one movement to indicate a mood, and it takes time to learn what these combination movements mean. It helps to be aware of subtle differences so you know when a situation is escalating. For example, a wagging tail is not just a sign of friendliness—a slow, intense wag can indicate fear or agitation.

Although most of us would be hard put to describe the canine body language that indicates an aggressive, upset dog, we know what it is when we see it. It's meant to be frightening, and that's the reaction people have.

Aggressive: The mouth and lips are open, teeth are exposed in a grimace, ears are almost flattened on the head, the body is tense, and the hackles (hair along the spine) are up. The dog is growling or barking, and the tail is straight out. This dog is in an aggressive mode and warning you to back off. The narrowed eyes issue a challenge. This is the height of danger for people.

Anxious: Unlike an aggressive posture, the anxious posture has ears partially back instead of flattened; the dog whines instead of growls, and the eyes are slightly narrowed. While the body is tense, it is lowered into a somewhat submissive position, and the tail is lowered a bit.

Alert: This can escalate into "aggressive" rather rapidly, but it's still a step down. The ears are still up, mouth is slightly open. He might be standing on tiptoe to be ready to move into aggression. The tail is up and wagging slowly.

Fearful: The ears are flat against the head, as in the aggressive posture, but the ears are narrowed down, and the dog's eyes are averted. His lips are drawn back to expose teeth. His body is tense and crouched into a submissive position, and his tail is between his legs. This posture is often accompanied by a low vocalization of some type.

A happy, friendly dog will have body language very different from one who is not.

Friendly: Ears are up, the body is relaxed, lips are relaxed, eyes are wide open, and the dog looks at you directly. His hind end may wiggle in greeting, and his tail is up. He'll be smiling, and you may or may not see his teeth, but the jaw is slack and relaxed.

Playful: The body is in a similar state of relaxation as in the friendly posture, but the dog is more active, jumping around, play-bowing, tail wagging, and jumping up, down, and all around. The tail is whipping around in excitement. He may circle around you, then run forward and back as part of his invitation to play.

Submissive: Although there are many ways to show submissive behavior, such as peeing excitedly when greeting new people, one basic piece of body language to show submission is for a dog to raise a front paw while bending the "knee."

Your Body Language: Don't kid yourself—dogs read body language better than most people do, both in other dogs and people. All those people who come home to a destroyed house and say "He knows he was bad, he slunk away" are actually misreading the cues. The dog has seen your body language as you step into the disaster that was once your kitchen, and he is reacting to your body language and mood shift. They are very sensitive to moods, which may be why so many dogs are sympathetic when you're feeling down.

If you want to train your dog, you must learn how to get his attention.

"Otto, sit."

The physical movement of raising his head to look at the treat will make his back end plop into the sit position. The *moment* he sits, give him the treat while praising him enthusiastically. Repeat—a lot.

Reinforce this useful command by having your dog sit for dinner, treats, while you put on his leash, or before you go out the door.

Down

Down is not as natural a position for dogs as Sit is. Dogs like to lie down well enough on their own when they feel like it, but they're not necessarily happy campers at being *asked* to go into this vulnerable position. This vulnerability is both physical and psychological, so some dogs accept the command more easily than do others. Begin teaching Down after your Miniature Schnauzer can sit on command. As with most training, there is more than one way to accomplish this. Food works miracles in training, because most Miniature Schnauzers are food motivated.

Tell your dog to sit while you hold a treat in your hand. As he is sitting, hold your hand so that he can see it contains a treat. Lower your hand to the floor in front of his legs and slowly pull that hand backward.

Another method is to kneel on the ground next to him. While facing him, put your left hand over his right foreleg and your right hand over his left foreleg. Gently pull his legs forward while you say "Otto, down."

No matter which method or combination of methods works best, don't force him into the Down. With either approach, it helps to pet him and stroke his back once he is in the down position, thus reinforcing that the down position is comfortable.

Stand

The Stand is a good behavior for Miniature Schnauzers to learn because it is useful during grooming as well as when visiting the vet. Whatever position your dog happens to be in, hold out a treat to him, say "Otto, stand," and raise it slowly to the level where his face will be when he's standing up. He'll go for the treat and stand up to do it. Once he's standing, keep the treat close to his nose as incentive. Let him have the treat the moment he's standing.

Heel (Walk on Leash)

Heeling occurs when your dog walks nicely by your side, as opposed to jumping around, criss-crossing in front of you, and causing you to trip over the leash. It's called heeling because the point is for the dog to walk positioned next to your left heel.

It doesn't really matter on which side your dog walks, but if you plan to engage in formal obedience training, you might as well start practicing walking on the left from the beginning. In agility, however, being on either side of the handler is necessary, so incorporate both sides if you wish to participate in both sports.

Keep the loop of the leash in your right hand but hold it and control it with your left hand, placing your hand about halfway down the length of the leash, leaving a bit of slack. Start by keeping a little treat in your left hand. Your dog will understand that staying close yields a reward; for a Miniature Schnauzer, this reward typically involves food, but he also thrives on praise. You want him to walk calmly at your side, not in front of you or behind you. When you stop walking, ask him to sit.

Once your dog knows the meaning of the Stand command, you can ask him to do it in a variety of places and circumstances.

Come (Recall)

No single other behavior is as important as having

your dog come to you when you call him. It can save his life, it can save you frustration, and it can save hours or days of being lost. It is really a critical command to teach.

One sunny afternoon, my dogs were out in the fenced backyard while I talked to a neighbor. I looked up and saw one of my dogs walking right in front of a raccoon that looked drunk. Thankfully, when I called the dog, she came running to me despite the distraction of an enticing new critter. The raccoon with distemper was euthanized in my yard that afternoon by animal control. Thankfully, the raccoon did not touch my dog because she came when I called her. Her good recall may have saved her life or at least prevented a traumatic wound and illness.

You want to associate good things with coming when called. When your dog comes bounding back to you, he gets a treat, not a nail trim or a pill. If you plan to do something to him that he considers unpleasant or distasteful, get up and go get him, or he'll associate your calling him with things he wants to run from. Obviously, you never, ever want to call your dog to you to punish him. His recall will never be the same, and it will always be filled

When teaching the Come command, start with your dog on a leash so that he doesn't have far to go and can't get too distracted.

with hesitation.

Start by working inside, in one room. It helps to start training Come when the dog is a puppy, but it can be done with adults. Call him by name— "Otto, come"—and show him that you have a treat in your hand. When he walks over to you, praise him like crazy. Don't reach for him, especially if he's a shy or timid dog. If he's shy, kneel down.

If he doesn't want to come, despite the tasty morsel in your hand, leash him and then say "Otto, come." Very gently pull the leash toward you. When he starts taking baby steps toward you, respond positively with praise, and offer a treat when he arrives at your feet. Use positive body language, such as opening your arms to him.

When he can do a reliable recall in a room, move outdoors to a fenced area. Use a short leash and repeat the

You may want to take training your Mini Schnauzer to the next level so that he can learn more precision work, like heeling no matter what speed you walk. That's impressive!

previous steps. When your dog displays that he has grasped the concept despite the distraction of being outdoors, switch to a longer 6-foot (1.8-m) leash (not a flexi) and slowly step away from him while calling his name. Hopefully, he will see it as an extension of what he's already done, and he will come to you.

Make sure he's reliable on the long lead before trying it off lead, because you never want to be in the position of having to chase him or call him to come when he is taking off in the opposite direction. Chasing a dog creates trouble; you will never run as fast as a terrier, and running around with your person who is making lots of fun noises is considered a great game to a dog. It's a game you want to avoid, however, because it places the dog in charge of what occurs between the two of you.

Practice frequently, not on just a weekly basis, but several times each day. After your dog has impressed you with his steadfast ability to do a solid recall for 2 or 3 weeks straight, try it without a leash in a safe, fenced area like your neighbor's yard or a fenced, empty dog park. Increase the level of distractions. When he comes to you when called, despite distractions, other dogs, playing kids, and somebody's picnic spread on the park table, you will have established a successful recall.

TRAINING FOR OBEDIENCE COMPETITION

Training your dog for formal obedience competition is a lot of fun, and it has the practical benefit of being a truly bonding experience. You will work with your dog as a team toward a given goal, whether your goal is to win a competition or to improve every time you compete.

Obedience trials test your dog's ability to do a given set of exercises in a specific manner. These trials are considered a sport, as well they should be.

Most kennel club chapters offer obedience classes designed specifically for people who want to compete in the sport. These classes are not the same as those designed for people who don't want their dogs to leap out of the car when the door is opened. These formal classes train you and your dog to do specific obedience exercises at the level in which you will compete.

TRAINING WITH THE WHOLE FAMILY

The reality of training is that, if you are the only human in the house, you are the only one who is going to have an impact on the training. Your consistency and effort will determine your Miniature Schnauzer's behavior. They are smart little dogs, and training them is quite simple, because they also like to please (despite being a tad stubborn sometimes).

However, when a couple lives in the house, your smart little Miniature Schnauzer will quickly realize that he can get away with something with Dad that he cannot get away with in front of Mom, or vice versa. Like little kids, your Mini Schnauzer is smart enough to know who is the softie, who is the disciplinarian, and how to skirt the edge of an issue. If Mom makes him Sit, Down, and then Stand for a treat each and every time, and Dad just pulls it out of the box and throws it, he will soon blow off respect for Dad because he knows Dad is far more. . .shall we say, flexible?. . . than Mom.

Length of Training Sessions

When puppies are very young, keep their training sessions short, no more than 5 minutes at a time. Their attention spans aren't quite in gear yet, and when they're older, they'll be able to concentrate better during longer training periods.

And he'll think of himself as more alpha than flexible old Dad who gives away all those free treats.

The scenario of who lets the dog get away with what increases exponentially when children and in-laws also live in the house. He will figure out exactly what he can get away with under the supervision of some, while knowing who he has to behave for (typically Mom or Dad). The person who takes the dog to training class most of the time is most likely to be the disciplinarian, and those who don't let him get away with freebies.

Ideally, everyone in the family should go to obedience class with the dog at least once in a while so they get the idea of what's happening there and why consistency is so important. If they don't attend, it's up to the person taking him to convey to family members why consistency is important and why it's critical that he not get freebies. Everyone must know that the dog doesn't get anything for free, and that he must see people as the repositories of his resources.

Training should be a family affair, or your dog might take advantage of the less knowledgeable or more "flexible" members of the family.

CRATE TRAINING

Crate training is popular in the United States and rather unpopular in Europe. In the United States, it's seen as an excellent aid for housetraining, a place to feed, a spot that each dog can call his own, and a safe place for the dog to stay while you're not at home. It's also a great place for recuperating dogs to stay when they require enforced rest.

In Europe, crates are not used for housetraining or sleeping. Many Europeans think that leaving a dog in a crate all day while you're at work is unconscionable. In some European countries, it is against the law to crate a dog for an extended period of time, and leaving the dog in a crate while you're at work would be breaking that law. Some dogs are suited to crates, and some aren't. It depends on their individual temperament. For starters, it's significantly easier for a dog to adapt to a crate while in puppyhood than it is to adapt to it as an adult.

Most Miniature Schnauzers will have to be in a crate, even minimally, at some point in their lives, and being crated at the groomer's and the veterinarian's is fairly certain. If you fly with your dog, he'll have to be crated. If you get evacuated in an emergency, such as a hurricane, a crate is a safe place for him.

One good reason to use crates is to protect your Schnauzer and your belongings during his teething stage, a time when he may feel inclined to chew and swallow door moldings, book bindings, your favorite pair of shoes, underwear, foam stuffing from your other dog's bed, items left on the floor, electric cables, curtains, remote controls, computer wires, your new cell phone, and—well, you know the drill. Mouthing puppies explore the world with their mouths and have no clue that swallowing a nail isn't a good idea; it's just one more thing to taste and explore. Leaving him in a crate can protect your dog from himself while you're not there to supervise.

When a crate is a pleasant place, your Miniature Schnauzer won't mind being in it; in fact, it may be his favorite getaway.

A crate is also a safe spot for your dog when he is riding in the car with you, because he won't be able to race around the car, get under the brake, and bark wildly out the window. (Author Stephen King was critically injured, almost fatally, when another driver was trying to control his loose dog in the back seat and not paying attention to driving.)

Once your Schnauzer reaches adulthood, you should be able to leave him alone in the house while you are gone, so that using the crate is a choice rather than a necessity.

Too Much of a Good Thing

Sadly, too many people overdo a good thing and use crates for far too many hours each day, turning the crate into a prison. An adult dog should not stay in a crate for more than 8 hours at a stretch, and puppies under 6 months of age should not be in one for more than 3 or 4 hours at a time; their little bladders and bowels just can't handle longer.

No dog will do well jammed into a crate all day while you're at work, let out only to be fed and go for a walk, and then jammed back into the crate while you go to a meeting, out for an hour while you get ready for bed, and then back into the crate for nighttime sleeping. That schedule is not only inappropriate but could cause bad traits to develop in your dog's formerly nice temperament.

If your dog keeps urinating and defecating in his crate, despite most dogs' inherent preference for keeping their sleeping area clean, you're going to have clean up, health, and emotional concerns, not to mention housetraining ones.

Even the little bit of physical activity that a dog gets in the house is beneficial compared to getting nothing at all. (For some elderly or ill Schnauzers, that may be all that's good for them.) No movement for hours on end is bad for dogs physically and mentally.

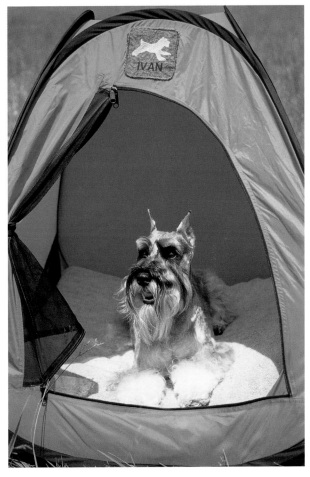

Once your dog knows the request for going into his crate, you can substitute other kinds of safe enclosures and use the same words to have him get inside them.

Introducing the Crate

Crate training should be done bit by bit, so that your dog becomes acclimated. It is stressful for you to put him in a crate for the first time while you go to work all day; he first needs to log some time in there at shorter intervals to make him comfortable with it. Start with crate placement: Put it in a place that is commonly used by the family, such as the family room, so that it is in a room your dog likes.

Encourage him to enter the crate by tossing some small treats near it, then just into it past the door, and then all the way in the back. Do not force him to go into the crate; rather, let him think it's his idea. For the first few times he is in the crate, praise him in a

Limit your puppy to areas that are easy to clean up in case he has an accident.

happy voice.

Start with really short periods during which you leave the room he's in, like for 10 minutes, before coming back to let him out. Repeat this multiple times during the first couple days of crate training. Once your Schnauzer can stay 30 minutes in the crate with you in the other room, and you know he is okay in there, then you can start leaving the house for short periods while he's crated. Teach him whatever command you like that tells him it's time to go into the crate, such as "Otto, crate" or "Kennel up."

One easily avoidable mistake is to not get emotional during either your coming or going. Don't say "Oh my gosh, poor Otto, I'll be back as soon as I can, you poor sad thing!" or "Otto, I've missed you desperately the past 2 hours, I'm so sorry I left you alone!" This level of emotion only exacerbates his worry or possible dislike of being left in the crate. You do him no favors with that kind of carrying on (or yourself, either). Staying calm and unemotional while coming and going is a good idea for everyone.

It's also possible that your last Miniature Schnauzer crated perfectly, but your new dog has problems with it. Don't let him hear your frustration or anger, or it will exacerbate the situation. Your new dog is not the same as your last dog, and he will not have the same reactions to things as she did. Just because they're the same breed doesn't mean they are exactly the same.

HOUSETRAINING

No other aspect of living with dogs produces such frustration and as many questions as housetraining. At 8 weeks of age, your Miniature Schnauzer is like a sponge waiting to soak up the world while he is busy soaking it with pee. It's time to begin teaching the basics of housetraining.

For the most part, Miniature Schnauzers are smart and efficient and will pick up the idea of housetraining readily, even though dogs clearly do not understand why *we* can pee in the house and they can't. They see no reason not to do it in the house except that you don't like it, even though there are lots of big, convenient rooms and empty places to go inside.

Keep the puppy in the same room with you any time he is awake. Choose whatever phrase you're going to use to tell him it's time to go, such as "Go potty." The trick is to use it *only* when you are outside and at the spot where you wish your puppy to go. Don't say it while you're still indoors or while carrying him outside.

When the puppy goes in the correct place, praise him to high heaven, gleefully and with a happy sing-song tone in your voice, or give him a treat that you have hidden away in a pocket. But don't let him see the treat before he goes potty.

It helps to have your puppy eat and drink at scheduled times when housetraining. Puppies need to go right after feeding and immediately upon waking up. If you're crate training, don't put water in the crate until he is fully housetrained. If food goes in at the same time on a daily basis, waste is going to come out at the same time on a daily basis. Once you've figured out these times, housetraining will be a lot easier for you.

Whether or not a puppy gives you cues, take him outside about once an hour and praise him if he goes. Puppies need to be about 16 weeks of age before you can expect them to have reasonable control of their bodily functions. Some dogs take longer than others to grasp the concept of housetraining; some dogs need more time than others to achieve muscular control of their systems.

Marking: Canine Instant Messaging

Dogs mark their territory by urinating on it. Most marking is done by males, but many females do it too. Marking has a purpose: It establishes presence. Your dog may mark his territory by urinating on a specific spot, often one that has just been marked by another dog. The marking indicates both that the dog was at that spot ("Kilroy was here") and that he is marking this territory as his. ("Mine, mine, mine!") If Otto marks Aunt Sally's suitcase, he is just letting Aunt Sally the Intruder know that this is his house.

Marking is different from plain old urinating in that it is just a tiny bit of urine rather than emptying the entire bladder. Testosterone directly affects the behavior, and neutered males are less likely to do it. Alpha females mark frequently too. Leg lifting is a dominant version of urine marking, and the urine is usually seen on vertical surfaces. However, it doesn't have to be vertical to constitute urine marking.

Done indoors, urine marking is usually a sign of stress or anxiety. Sometimes indoor marking is a reaction to something like a new baby or pet, or a reflection of overall stress in the household. Punishment is inappropriate for this stress-related problem and will only worsen it.

Prevention Versus Punishment

As with any form of dog training, it is easier to prevent bad habits than to correct them. Housetrain your Miniature Schnauzer with positive reinforcement rather than screaming "NOOOOOO!" as you bolt in a frenzy toward the poor dog.

All dogs, even intelligent Miniature Schnauzers, will make some mistakes during housetraining. The most critical thing to remember during housetraining is that if you don't see your dog go in the house, if you don't catch him in the act, do not respond to it. Do not tell him he's a bad dog and that he made a mistake. He will have no clue what you're talking about, because he has no ability to connect the poop he left 3 minutes ago with what you're upset about now.

The only way he will understand why you're upset is if you catch him in the act and tell him while he's doing it. Conversely, when he goes where you want him to go, whether it's anywhere outside or on a specific bit of ground, praise him to high heavens *as he goes*, not after.

Thus, the critical components of housetraining are to only react to an indoor accident if you see it happening, not after, and to praise highly when he goes where you want him to go. That's housetraining in a nutshell. Learn to pay close attention to his cues to you that indicate his need to go.

Alternate Options

Some people like to first train their dog to go on newspapers or scented piddle pads in the house, and then move the training outside. The problem with this approach is that you have to train one way, move the location, and train again in a different way, which is untraining the first method.

Usually it's easier to just start with outside training. However, if you live in a high-rise, getting outside quickly is a real problem and using the paper method is understandable and possibly an easier option. Some people use cat litter boxes filled with special litter for dogs, but that works best for very tiny toy dogs; Miniature Schnauzers are a bit big for it.

To facilitate any method of housetraining, try using a crate because dogs prefer not to soil their sleeping quarters.

Housetraining an Adult

If you found your Miniature Schnauzer at the shelter or through Miniature Schnauzer rescue, you may need to housetrain an adult dog. It may be a matter of reinforcing what seems to have been neglected, or it may be teaching the dog all over again, especially if he was left outside too much. Use positive reinforcement only; this is not a situation for negative reinforcement.

The process is exactly the same as housetraining a puppy except that your adult dog already has a strong bladder and bowel, unless a medical condition is present.

LEASH TRAINING

A dog must be on a leash sometimes. Even if you have a huge fenced rural area, he still needs a leash when you go to the vet, dog school, or the local dog park.

Start by getting your puppy used to a collar. After putting on the collar for the first time, distract him with something fun like toys, a treat, or dinner. Puppies often fight the collar, but if you take it off while he is fussing with it, you'll reinforce that he doesn't have to wear it when he doesn't want to. He'll eventually get used to it, just as you get used to wearing a new piece of jewelry.

Once your Miniature Schnauzer has adjusted to the collar and doesn't fuss over it, add in the leash. Sometimes it helps to start out with a fake leash that is significantly lighter in weight than a real leash, such as a shoelace or piece of yarn.

Enzymatic Cleaner

Have some enzymatic cleaner on hand for your floors. If you do not fully eliminate the odor of urine, your dog will be inclined to return to that spot, since it's already marked and he thinks it must be okay to go there even if it is inside the house.

It may take some time for your dog to adjust to his collar and leash, but he will.

Again, distract him while attaching the fake leash, and play with him. Feed him while he's wearing it so that he knows good things happen when he's wearing it. He has yet to discover the joys of neighborhood walks! After he's used to the fake leash, attach the real leash, but don't pull on it yet.

Then, when he's comfortable with the real leash draping behind him, pick it up in your hand and let him know that you are at the other end. Your dog will soon learn that a leash connects him to you.

Keep the leash loose, although that is often easier said than done. Pulling on the leash makes for unpleasant walks for you, and it's tough on your dog's throat. A significant part of your leash training is to keep the leash loose.

When he goes too fast and pulls the leash, either stop or straighten your arm and change directions with an about-face. You may feel a little odd taking a 30-minute walk in a 10-foot (3.0-m) circle at the end of your driveway, but the effort will pay off. If you give in and walk while your Schnauzer is pulling the leash, it will be much harder to train him not to do it. Train him correctly from the start, and your life will be much easier.

Adults in need of leash training require patience and take a little more work than a puppy does, but it's the same approach. Changing directions usually works better for adults. You don't want to teach him that a tight leash is normal or okay.

Get excited and happy and ask him to follow you: "Come on, Otto, let's go!" Be free with the treats. Later, your dog will see the benefits of a leash—like going on walks—and you won't need treats.

SOCIALIZATION

Few components of a puppy's growth period are as critical as socialization. The more varied situations to which your puppy is exposed, the more confident he will be as an adult.

No matter what your Miniature Schnauzer's genetics are, lots of socializing as a puppy gives the best chance for your dog to have a well-rounded personality and good social skills. Good breeding is not enough; you must provide sufficient exposure to the outside world.

Puppies must be exposed not only to a variety of people, but to other dogs, animals, and places as well. Miniature Schnauzers are generally quite social, and they like animals, children, and other dogs. They're easy to socialize, because it is natural to them; they are not happy without people.

Puppies learn a lot from their mother and their littermates. Littermates learn to socialize with people as a group, which is good for them. Good breeders introduce litters to a variety of people, including children.

The prime socialization timeframe is from approximately 7 to 14 weeks (about 2 to 4 months). One particularly critical period in your puppy's life is the fear stage, which usually begins around the age of 8 to 10 weeks and lasts until the puppy is about 12 weeks old. Unfortunately, these two periods overlap. After 14 weeks of age,

Puppies need a supply of appropriate and safe toys to prevent certain problems behaviors, like chewing.

puppies become more suspicious of their surroundings, and the more they've been socialized, the more confident they will be as adults.

What happens in those early, formative weeks and months affects the rest of your dog's life. It's not how many experiences they have that matters most, but whether or not those experiences are negative or positive that makes the difference. The more experiences they have, the more likely they will be to have good rather than bad experiences outside the home.

Where to Go

Puppy class is a huge boon to socialization, and it is highly recommended by trainers, although some veterinarians have concerns about exposing puppies to other animals before the puppy is fully vaccinated. Puppy kindergarten is kind of like a large group play date, and the goal is more about socialization and playing with peers than about training.

Some puppy kindergarten classes do cover basic commands like Sit and Stay. Puppies at this age soak up training and knowledge. And instructors can help with such puppy behaviors as mouthing and jumping up.

If you are concerned about exposure to disease, instead of puppy kindergarten, arrange frequent play dates for your puppy with dogs you know are vaccinated and who are willing and well-behaved enough to play with a puppy.

An Ongoing Process

The need for socialization does not end at the onset of adulthood. Socialization is something that should continue throughout the dog's life, although probably not as intensely as with a puppy.

Adult Miniature Schnauzers need new experiences to keep sharp (and they're born smart). Adult socialization activities include frequent interaction with people and dogs not in your family, play dates with children and other dogs, walks around the neighborhood where you stop and chat with neighbors, and trips to the dog park or other places where dogs are allowed on leash. They also must have good experiences with people who come to your home.

As your Miniature Schnauzer becomes a senior citizen, he still needs socializing. Although he may not be as interested in it as he once was, he will still enjoy trips out and being with others.

Special Issues

Puppies who are taken away from their litter too soon sometimes have a tough time interacting with other dogs. Many of these puppies can become either shy or aggressive adults, particularly if not socialized.

Puppies, even outgoing happy ones, can become nervous and fearful of almost everything. During the anxious fear period, continue to socialize your puppy, but do what you can to control the interactions and ensure that they are all positive.

For example, take him to a play date with one dog who you know and trust, as opposed to going to the dog park where you don't know who you'll run into that afternoon. Introduce him to one person at a time instead of a family. You will not be able to control every situation—an unexpected loud noise during this period can elicit a fear response—but do what you can.

PROBLEM BEHAVIORS

Left uncurbed, some natural canine behaviors can be problematic for people. Miniature Schnauzers are terriers and thus want to dig (go to ground) and bark. Chewing is a natural behavior for teething dogs, but some dogs keep it up as a stress reliever. It helps to understand that these are natural behaviors, and your dog is not trying to be spiteful or troublesome—he's just being a terrier. It's not like he has any choice about whether or not to be a terrier.

One important thing to remember is the most useful adage for dog owners: A tired dog is a good dog. Many problem behaviors result from either boredom or lack of exercise. Giving your

Abnormal Behavior

What is abnormal behavior for a dog, as opposed to unwanted behavior?

Biting, lunging, growling at people, or any type of aggressive behavior is not normal. Neither is an overly timid, shy dog who hides under furniture rather than deal with the world. Adult hyperactive dogs who cannot focus or pay attention for more than a few moments are not normal, although they must be differentiated from plain old high-energy dogs (and Miniature Schnauzers can certainly be high-energy dogs). Constant barking, whining, or crying is problematic and not considered normal.

Abnormal behaviors can be addressed by a canine behaviorist.

Miniature Schnauzer enough exercise is critical if you want to live with a calm dog.

Barking

Barking can be a significant problem with Miniature Schnauzers, and it is one of the more common reasons for them to be turned into rescue. Barking is instinctive. Schnauzers are naturally quite barky, and if this instinct is not curbed early in life, it can be difficult to work with.

Dogs who bark enough to disturb the neighborhood regularly can result in the police showing up on your doorstep as a result of neighbor complaints. Your neighbors have a right to live in peace and not hear your dog bark all the time, just as you have a right not to hear the dog next door bark his fool head off all night and day.

Barking while indoors is less likely to bother the neighbors than barking outdoors, so keeping your dog indoors most of the time makes a positive difference. It can also help if you are outside when

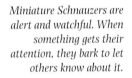

Miniature Schnauzers are alert and watchful. When something gets their attention, they bark to let others know about it.

your dog is. You will be aware of when he starts barking, and you can stop it when it starts.

First, check out what your dog is barking about, which could range from a crew of burglars to a bee flying by. A friend of mine once ignored the usual barkfest from her dogs and discovered the next morning that her Mercedes had been stolen from her driveway.

Next, back away from where you're standing and call your dog to you. Treat him for coming. You may need to do this several times in a row, but eventually he'll get the idea that it pays not to bark. Your Schnauzer is also smart enough to get the idea that if he barks inside you'll treat him, so vary the reward with treats and praise so that he doesn't learn to bark just to get a treat. Petting helps too.

Stopping the barkfest means you have stopped the adrenaline rush that comes with it. Barking for some dogs can induce a high, and they can get addicted to the excitement of it. Halting the positive benefit they get from barking helps break the pattern.

Another tactic, best used indoors, is to put coins in an empty soda can and shake it near the dog when he is barking too much. The noise bothers most dogs enough so that they stop barking. This is not effective with every dog, but it's worth a try.

One solution to barking at people and other dogs you see while out on walks is to distract your Miniature Schnauzer with treats and behaviors such as sitting or turning around, which stimulates his mind. A tightly held leash increases the dog's defensive attitude—which may increase the barking—so keep the leash loose.

Chewing

All puppies chew when they're teething, which usually occurs around 4 to 6 months of age. (This is approximate timing, and some puppies will chew earlier or later than that.) Some people have lost entire couches to teething puppies, while some have just lost a few pieces of paper that were on the floor. Gums and jaws hurt when the teeth come in, and chewing helps relieve the discomfort of teething.

You can soak some rags in water and freeze them so that your Miniature Schnauzer has something cold on which to chew, or buy a canine teething ring that is first placed in the freezer. Get one designed for a dog, not a baby, because a puppy can chew a lot harder than a baby can, and he may break the ring.

The frightening part about this perfectly natural chewing behavior is that dogs can choke on objects that they are trying to chew. During your puppy's teething stage, keep an eye on what your puppy is doing to prevent choking problems.

Dogs who are not teething generally chew to relieve stress or boredom. Highly intelligent dogs like Miniature Schnauzers get bored easily without sufficient intellectual stimulation and may turn to chewing for entertainment. In some cases, for an only dog, the answer may be a second dog with whom he can play.

Make sure your dog has plenty of safe chew toys. When you find him chewing on something that he shouldn't, trade the object for one of his chew toys. If you just pull the inappropriate object out of his mouth, it may increase his desire for it, so trading is better.

Train him to know which items are his to chew. Don't let him have your old slippers because he can't differentiate between old slippers you don't use anymore and your favorite new ones.

If you find your dog chewing on something he shouldn't, say "Otto, no chew," lead him to his toys, and hand him one in exchange for the item you don't want him to chew. When your dog starts playing with it, say "Otto, good boy!" Rotate the toys once in a while, and get new ones regularly to keep interest up.

Sad to say, for some people, this is one dog behavior issue where housekeeping skills come into play. If you own an item you absolutely do not want your dog to get his teeth on, do not allow it to be accessible. Keeping things off the floor makes a big difference. (If you have small children at home, this is easier said than done.)

Digging

Miniature Schnauzers are earth-bound terriers, bred to burrow into the ground after vermin. They like digging. Digging is hard-wired into terriers, and eliminating this behavior is probably not possible.

That doesn't mean you lack options. While your dog is not likely to dig to China, he may easily dig under the fence and get out. It's quite a jolt to look out the front window and see your dog jogging down the street by himself. One remedy is to create aversions, such as laying chicken wire flat in the area you don't want him to dig, although the behavior will probably transfer to another spot in the yard. Try selecting an area in your yard where your Schnauzer *is*

Why Do Dogs Dig?

If your dog is male and is unaltered, part of the digging may be wanderlust associated with testosterone, in which case neutering may help alleviate some of the problem. Seeing prey wander by on the other side of the fence makes some dogs work hard to get out of the fence by digging. Boredom and lack of intellectual stimulation, sheer lack of fun, need for attention, and need of exercise can contribute to a desire to dig like crazy. Addressing these issues may help alleviate the digging problem.

allowed to dig. Think in terms of a sandbox. Fence it with something like chicken wire or garden fencing, mark a specific area that has boundaries, and cover it with loose soil.

Train your dog to dig on command in the place you choose. This may take a few weeks, during which time you must be with him every time he is outside—supervision is essential.

Start out by "planting" treats, toys, or both in the area. Let your Miniature Schnauzer see you plant them. Don't plant them too deeply; you might even want to leave part of a treat sticking out of the dirt in the beginning. Praise him when he uses this spot to dig, and give a command "Otto, dig."

Leave your dog inside while you plant a treat, and then let him find it. When he starts to dig elsewhere, say something like "No dig. Dig in Otto's spot." Walk your dog to his area and say "Otto, dig." Miniature Schnauzers are so intelligent that soon your dog will be digging only where he is allowed.

Jumping on Furniture

Before your Miniature Schnauzer sets even one paw inside your home, have everyone who lives there agree on whether or not the dog will be allowed on all furniture, some of it (specify which furniture), or none.

Abide by these decisions, or you will be inconsistent. A Miniature Schnauzer sees your inconsistency as lack of leadership, and he will take advantage of these inconsistencies. If the dog is not allowed on some furniture, never let him up there even for a minute. If he tries to get up, shoo him off.

Separation Anxiety

Separation anxiety is fairly common in adult dogs who come from shelter or rescue. As with most transplanted adults, they

develop a very strong bond with their people and often feel stressed at the idea of not being with them because they are afraid of more separation. These dogs may follow you from room to room. Some changes, such as a move or death of pet or human in the family, may make the struggle more difficult.

Dogs with separation anxiety tend to have a distress response within approximately 20 to 45 minutes after they are left alone. Some dogs chew or scratch at doors so much that they cause damage. Some bark or cry most of the time they are left alone, provoking valid complaints from neighbors. Even housetrained dogs have been known to have accidents while left alone. For these dogs, nothing is more stressful than being left alone.

If the problem is rooted in separation anxiety, one approach is to make your comings and goings unemotional. When you leave the house, don't make a fuss and tell your dog how much you're going to miss him. When you come back, rather than leap right to him saying "Otto, doggy, light of my life, I missed you so much while I was at the grocery store," ignore him for the first few minutes. Too much emotion attached to coming and going increases stress. Not making any fuss is easier on your dog in the long run.

Sometimes separation anxiety is a short-term thing, such as when your Miniature Schnauzer comes home from being boarded at the kennel and clings to you. Or if you have spent every waking moment of a vacation together, the change back to a workday schedule can precipitate separation anxiety. Schnauzers are extremely people-oriented, and if they haven't had enough attention, they may react with anxiety.

For these short-term episodes, it helps to give your dog clothing with your scent on it while you are gone. Leaving the television or radio on also can provide comfort. Getting another dog may or may not help; because the anxiety is produced by separation from you, adding a second dog may not do the trick. For some dogs, however, another dog is just the ticket.

Desensitization

Desensitization techniques can be useful for separation anxiety. Desensitization is a method that exposes a dog, bit by increasing bit, to whatever scares him, thus slowly desensitizing him to his fears.

For example, pretend you are leaving. Get ready the way you

normally do, get your coat, keys, and such, and then leave and lock the door. Come back in several seconds. Repeat, except increase the amount of time you are gone each time. Keep increasing the length of the absences, and don't fall into a pattern of when to do it. Do it intermittently, sometimes several times in an afternoon, or once in the evening. Try to avoid having the dog know what you're doing.

As emphasized repeatedly, Miniature Schnauzers are very smart, and it won't take them long to figure out that you're not really gone if you stand on the other side of the door. Walk away from the door. Once you get to the point where your dog can stay alone for 30 to 60 minutes without a problem, you are probably safe in leaving him for longer periods.

Doggie day care can be a real boon for dogs with separation anxiety. They will have lots of socialization and exercise, and learn to have a good time when you're not around, thus reducing their emotional dependence on you. Plenty of exercise helps stave off obsessive behavior, so lots and lots of exercise helps stressed-out dogs. Remember, a tired dog is a good dog.

Medications are available for severe cases. Anti-anxiety meds are not new in veterinary medicine and include medications such as clomipramine (Clomicalm) or amitriptyline hydrochloride (Elavil). However, if you can alleviate the problem with behavior

Being left alone can be stressful for dogs. With a comfy bed and a companion, these Mini Schnauzers can rest easy while their owner is away.

modification, you can avoid possible side effects from medications as well as the cost.

If your dog is so fearful while you are gone that you are afraid he might harm himself in his emotional frenzy, a crate can be a safe place—unless he hurts himself trying to get out. If your dog's anxiety is so bad that he tries to jump out closed windows, contact an animal behaviorist.

FINDING AN ANIMAL BEHAVIORIST

If you discover that your Miniature Schnauzer has problem behaviors that you and your obedience instructors are unable to solve, and your veterinarian says the problem doesn't have a physical basis, consider contacting an animal behaviorist. Any extreme change in behavior, or one that has been steadily deteriorating over time, calls for attention. Behaviorists have appropriate skills to work with the psychological aspects of significant problem behaviors. But how do you find a good one and not simply some dog lover who decided to throw up a shingle and go into business?

Ask around. Ask around obedience school, the dog park, and your friends. Get a recommendation from someone whose doggy opinions you respect. In this way, you have a better chance of liking the behaviorist than if you randomly pick one out of the phone book.

The International Association of Animal Behavior Consultants (IAABC) is a professional trade association of animal behaviorists that provides certification. Their mission is to educate animal owners "to interrupt the cycle of inappropriate punishment, rejection, and euthanasia of animals with resolvable behavior problems." Although most members are American, the IAABC's website has a locator service that provides a list of behaviorists by region in the United States, Canada, and Europe. IAABC members also

If your Mini Schnauzer begins to develop into more of a pest than a pleasant pet, it may be time to call a certified animal behaviorist.

work with cats, parrots, horses, and other animals.

Specialized and certified dog behavior consultant can evaluate and modify canine behaviors. The International Association of Dog Behavior Consultants (IADBC) is a division of IAABC. They help minimize stress in training and help the entire family train together consistently. They also understand that problem behaviors can be caused by medical issues. Prevention is emphasized.

Typically, certified dog behavior consultants work on such cases as dogs who are aggressive (toward people or other animals), excessive barking and digging, destructive behaviors, jumping, separation anxiety, shyness, obsessive behavior such as air snapping or excessive licking, and housetraining problems.

The consultant will come to your house, observe your dog in his normal surroundings, and watch how he interacts with family members. Once the behaviorist has identified the issues, she will help define goals and teach you training and/or behavior modification methods to achieve those goals.

Another option is to consult a veterinarian who is a diplomate of the American College of Veterinary Behaviorists. These veterinarians typically are also certified through IAABC.

ADVANCED TRAINING and ACTIVITIES

With Your Miniature Schnauzer

Whatever activities you enjoy, there's sure to be one you can do with your Miniature Schnauzer. The dog world is full of excitement and brims with activities, competitions, titles, fun matches, and other events. Competitive dog events are social and addictive. Participating in one type of activity often precedes a desire to participate in many of them.

If you decide to participate in a dog sport, your dog will be in much better physical shape than he would be as a couch potato who just takes neighborhood walks. Plus, he'll be well socialized around people and other dogs, and you will discover a joy unlike any other when the two of you work successfully together as a team.

THE CANINE GOOD CITIZEN PROGRAM

The AKC offers a basic test that was created to reward the good manners of a companion dog. We're not talking about skills for dogs competing in obedience or gaiting around a show ring. We're talking about dogs with nice manners who are a joy to live with and are not an embarrassment when out and about.

This test is a way of stressing responsible dog ownership and is the first formal goal for many people when training their dog. It serves as an excellent springboard for training in fun performance events like obedience or agility. The program emphasizes your dog's ability to walk under control, come when called (for some dogs, this is difficult to learn), stay in place, lie down, and sit on command.

The CGC certificate is awarded to purebreds and mixed breeds, so your Miniature Schnauzer mix is welcome. Spayed and neutered dogs are welcome too. During the test, pinch, prong, or electronic correction collars cannot be used. Be sure your dog is neatly groomed and clean. (He doesn't have to go to the groomer for this, but he should have had a bath recently and feel nice to touch.)

The Ten Stations

The CGC examination includes ten separate stations:

Acceptance and Grooming

Bring the brush you normally use at home on your dog and give that brush to the examiner, who then uses it on your dog. It's okay if he rolls over and gives the examiner his belly. They're not testing whether he stays still; what they really want to know is if he can go to the veterinarian or groomer and behave nicely.

Accepting a Stranger

The examiner shakes your hand while you stand next to your dog to test that he is neither afraid of a strange person or all over him with excessive exuberance.

Walk on a Loose Lead

This shows who is in control—you or your dog. While formal heeling is not part of this test, your dog must walk nicely on lead without pulling. You make a left turn, right turn, and about turn, as the examiner requests.

Walk Through a Crowd

Your dog is asked to walk the gauntlet—in other words—walk through a small group of people while paying more attention to you than to them. He should not show fear or aggression. Some of these people will purposely try to distract him by walking in front of him or dropping something.

Sit for Exam

Your dog must sit at your left side on your command. The examiner then walks up to him and pets him.

Sit and Down on Command

This shows you've had some formal training and that your dog responds to your commands. Unlike the formal obedience ring, during the test you can repeat these commands. Over and over and over, if need be. But you can't force the dog into either position, or you and your dog won't pass the test.

Coming When Called

While on a long, loose line, you walk 10 feet (3.0 m) or so away from your dog and call him to you. Until you call him, he must stay where he is. If your dog is more interested in that cute Basset Hound in line, you are allowed to use body language and encouragement to get him to come to you. ("Get over here, you darn dog!" is not considered appropriate encouragement.)

Reaction to Another Dog

Two handlers and their dogs approach each other. The people stop, shake hands, and then continue on. Neither dog should go to

Sports and Safety

Before you jump off the couch and into agility or freestyle, be sure that both you and your dog are in good enough physical condition to participate in these events. Neither you nor he can go directly from being couch potatoes to racing around a course at high speed without first getting into shape. As with human weekend warriors, you and your Schnauzer may pay for that kind of excess with preventable injuries and muscle strains.

If you walk your dog for a good distance every day, he should be in reasonably decent shape. If you run or jog with him regularly, he ought to be in great shape. If you let him run free every day in a safe area like a fenced dog park, he is probably in good shape.

The key is consistency. If you only run with your dog once every other weekend, then he could be prone to muscle sprains and strains, just as you would be if you only ran that infrequently. Build up to any sport by getting physically fit.

Before you embark on a training program for any kind of sport, have your vet make sure that your Mini is in good physical shape. Otherwise, you could unknowingly exacerbate an incipient health problem. Use common sense during training and competition, and don't overdo it, particularly in extreme temperatures and climates. Obviously, don't compete if either you or your dog is ill. Many competitive events require proof of vaccination, because the sheer number of dogs at a competition could become a breeding ground for something contagious, so have your paperwork handy.

A dog who is a Canine Good Citizen should be able to accept a friendly stranger—even one who is dressed unusually or who is carrying something unfamiliar.

the other handler or dog.

Reaction to Distractions

The examiner selects two of seven possible distractions, such as wheelchairs or dropping a book. Your Schnauzer must ignore the distractions.

Dog Left Alone

You hand your dog's leash to a test examiners and walk out of sight for a couple of minutes. He can move about a bit, but he can't show any distress through whining or barking.

Scoring

Dogs are evaluated on a pass/fail test, not on a curve. This isn't college. It doesn't matter if your dog almost didn't pass or was the best one tested in the last 6 years—he either passes or he doesn't.

Don't Give Up

Some of these exercises are easier said than done, and they take a lot of work. Some dogs have a tough time on a long stay. Some don't pass the test because they are too friendly to people or other dogs, can't stand to be separated from you, or don't do what they're told. A few hours of training is not enough to pass this test unless you have Super Dog. Even smart dogs like Miniature Schnauzers must be trained. The AKC recommends a 6-week training class to prepare.

Work with your Schnauzer over time, provide increasing levels of distraction, and don't give up if it doesn't come easily. If your dog only practices a long stay when no one else is around, he may not be able to do it in a room full of people and dogs. Train with him in different places and situations; go to friends' houses, the dog park, and the kennel club. Practice his Sit command at street corners while you walk him. Make him sit or down for treats.

Some dogs never pass the test. That doesn't mean you have a stupid Miniature Schnauzer; you might have a Miniature Schnauzer who trains you better than you train him. Failing just means that this particular dog didn't perform these tasks well enough on a given day to pass the test. It does not mean you have the dog from hell (although God knows you might).

Friendly handling, inspection, and grooming should all be accepted by dogs who are qualified to be Good Citizens.

THE GOOD CITIZEN DOG SCHEME

The Kennel Club's version of the Canine Good Citizen test is called the Good Citizen Dog Scheme. Like the CGC, this test is meant to promote responsible dog ownership in the United Kingdom, and it emphasizes that dog owners have an obligation to their community.

The Scheme has been just as successful as the CGC and is nationally recognized in Britain. It incorporates simple exercises in areas such as basic training, grooming, exercise, diet, cleaning up after your dog, and general health care. The test has four levels: bronze, silver, gold, and puppy foundation assessment. Each level is meant to gradually increase an owner's understanding of dogs.

All dogs, purebred or mix, altered or not, can participate in the noncompetitive Scheme.

Puppy Foundation

The goal here is to start educating your dog from a young age. Puppies as young as 10 weeks can begin

training. There are 12 basic components:

- Responsibility and care
- Cleanliness and identification
- Attentive response to name
- Puppy play
- Socialization
- Handling and inspection
- Puppy recall
- Basic puppy positions
- Walking in a controlled manner
- Stay for approximately 10 seconds
- Take article away from the puppy
- Food manners (take a treat without snatching)

Bronze

This level is quite similar to the CGC. The components include:

- Cleanliness and identification
- Collar and lead
- Walk on lead
- Control at door or gate
- Controlled walk among people and dogs
- Stay on lead for 1 minute
- Groom
- Present for examination
- Return to handler
- Responsibility and care

Silver

Dogs must pass the Bronze level before taking on the Silver. It tests the owner as much as it tests the dog.

- Play with the dog
- Road walk
- Stay in one place
- Vehicle control
- Come away from distractions
- Controlled greeting
- Food manners
- Examination of the dog
- Responsibility and care

Gold

The Kennel Club Good Citizen Gold Award is the highest level of Good Citizenship in the Scheme. Dogs must have earned a Silver Award before attempting the Gold.

- Road walk
- Return to handler's side
- Walk free beside handler
- Stay down in one place
- Send the dog to bed
- Stop the dog (before an emergency occurs)
- Relaxed isolation
- Food manners
- Examination of the dog
- Responsibility and care: This section tests the handler, not the dog. Topics about which the owner must be knowledgeable include other responsibilities; children; barking; dogs and stationary vehicles; vehicle travel; health; worming; the country code; frightening or out-of-control dogs; biting; and the psychology of canine learning.

THERAPY DOGS

Therapy dogs visit people in nursing homes, hospitals, and rehabilitation centers to brighten spirits. (Therapy work does wonders for the dogs' spirits, too.) Petting a dog reduces blood pressure and physical stress, so it helps ill patients heal.

Calm Miniature Schnauzers make lovely therapy dogs. They are so intuitively tuned in to people that they know when someone is not feeling well physically, or when they're feeling low. They are also small enough that they can cuddle in beds, sit on laps in wheelchairs, and help children who are afraid of big dogs. Senior dogs who may not be physically fit enough for sports competitions may well find that therapy is just the ticket.

Making a Difference

Therapy dogs can make a significant difference in someone's attitude during an illness or hospital stay. Residents of rest homes that have live-in therapy dogs or who are visited by therapy dogs tend to be happier and healthier. Being able to pet a dog takes people's thoughts away from focusing on themselves for a few moments, and it helps lower the high blood pressure related to the

A face like this can bring comfort and joy to those who may no longer be able to care for an animal.

stress of being ill or aging.

Children's hospitals that use therapy dog visits usually mention the program at admission. Having a dog nuzzle up to a child who is bald or has a lot of attached tubes helps that child attain some sense of normalcy, a sense that every minute of every day is not about being sick. Often, particularly for children, seeing dogs removes a lot of worry about what they look like while they're sick.

Many children and adults miss their dogs at home, and therapy dogs give them an opportunity to tell the handler about the dogs they miss. Just petting a dog makes people feel calmer; calmer people experience less stress than worried people and they heal faster. Think about what your reaction would be if you were sick and someone brought in their Miniature Schnauzer to see you: Wouldn't you forget your woes for a bit while petting such a gorgeous coat and looking at that lovely face?

Therapy dogs also visit rest homes or hospice centers where people don't expect to ever leave. In these situations, dogs bring a sense of joy and a fond remembrance of life to a dull routine that can have frightening moments. Dogs are vibrant and totally in the present moment. They don't worry about this afternoon, much less tomorrow. Dogs help people feel more in the moment too. For those facing interminable days in the hospital, or knowing they're never going to improve, these moments have great meaning and value.

You can take one of several approaches to doing therapy with your dog. Some areas have informal programs set up through their humane society. These programs connect people and their dogs with rest homes and rehabilitation centers. Some of these programs require formal certification by such national dog-therapy programs as Therapy Dogs International (TDI) or Delta Society, but some don't. Some specialized places like hospitals have their own programs set up. However, the best way to learn about doing therapy with your dog is to contact TDI or Delta. Additionally, some therapy-dog groups require that a dog passes the CGC test before applying for membership.

OBEDIENCE

As defined by the AKC, "Obedience trials test a dog's ability to perform a prescribed set of exercises on which it is scored." Miniature Schnauzers are very good in obedience because they like to please their people and are a natural in the obedience ring. Plus, advanced obedience gives your Schnauzer a chance to really use his brain.

The real joy, the true joy, of competing in obedience is the bonding that occurs between you and your dog while preparing for competition. You work as a team, and you know what to expect from each other. The sheer amount of one-on-one time involved in training builds a bond that becomes stronger during every training session.

One of the hardest things for dogs to accept—especially in populated areas like parks—is relaxed isolation.

AKC

The AKC has three levels of increasing difficulty at which a dog can earn a title: Novice, Open, and Utility. Each level may be split in half, with beginners entering "A" (people whose dogs have not yet won a title) and more experienced handlers going into "B" categories.

In each competition, your dog must score more than half of the available points (the amount differs per event, but ranges from 20 to 40) and get a minimum score of 170 out of 200 possible to qualify. If your dog gets 170 or higher, he has a leg toward a title. It takes three legs for your dog to win an obedience title. The scoring

is complex, but beginners who initially may be intimidated eventually start rattling off numerical scoring equations with ease.

The Novice level earns a Companion Dog (CD) title. Skills tested include heeling both off and on leash at different speeds, coming when called, staying quietly with a group of dogs, and standing up for a physical exam.

The second level is called Open, and in it, your dog can earn a Companion Dog Excellent (CDX) title. The exercises are pretty much the same as in Novice, with the addition of some jumping and retrieving tasks. These exercises, however, are done off leash and for longer periods of time.

Competitions at the Utility (UD) level are quite interesting to watch. These dogs perform more difficult exercises and need to demonstrate some scent-discrimination skills.

UD dogs can continue to compete at a higher level. They can work toward an Utility Dog Excellent (UDX) title, then go on for an Obedience Trial Champion (OTCH) title.

United Kennel Club (UKC)

The UKC offers pre-beginner, beginner, novice, open, A, B, and championship C classes. Scent discrimination is included, as well as distance control and obeying from a distance.

EARTHDOG TESTS

Earthdog sports test a dog's ability to follow game to ground and work the quarry. This is part of what Miniature Schnauzers are bred for, so they have an innate aptitude for it.

The basic idea behind "going to ground" is that the dog can follow prey into its den or burrow. Usually, the live quarry consists of two rats in a cage; the rats have food and water and are not hurt (although they are certainly alarmed, I suspect, and one wonders if any rat cardiologists are on call).

How, exactly, does an earthdog trial work? Your Miniature Schnauzer follows the scent of the rat down into a 9-inch by 9-inch (22.9-cm by 22.9-cm) tunnel in which the scent is already laid out. At the end of the tunnel is the den, which holds a cage with a couple of rats in it.

The dog "works the quarry" by barking and digging. Growling, lunging, and biting at the cage are also considered working the quarry. Really, it's getting worked up over the quarry to indicate interest; it's the one time you really want your terrier to make a lot of noise. Sitting there quietly and staring at the rats or having some kind of Star Trek mind meld with them is not considered to be working the quarry.

The den is, of course, a false den prepared by people. (It would be too hard to locate a field with real dens in convenient places.) It's just a pile of bedding material scented to simulate a natural den.

The AKC's introductory course for quarry work does not grant a title and is designed to give your dog a taste of what earthdog trials are all about. Dogs must be 6 months old to participate. They go through a short tunnel, 10 feet (3.0 m) in length, that has one 90-degree turn.

The first competitive trial is Junior Earthdog (JE), for which the tunnel is 30 feet (9.1 m) long and has three 90-degree turns. The Senior Earthdog (SE) also has a 30-foot (9.1-m) tunnel with three 90-degree turns, but adds in a false den and exit, and the owner has to call the Miniature Schnauzer out of the tunnel. The caged rats are taken out of the tunnel before the owner calls the dog.

The Master Earthdog (ME) title is granted for work in a 30-foot (9.1-m) tunnel with three 90-degree turns, one false entrance, a false den, and an exit. The tricky part here is that the dog must go to the correct entrance and has to let another dog work at the same time. Letting another dog work while your dog waits quietly is called *honoring another dog*, and it's no surprise that this is only found at the highest level of competition.

A tricky part of earthdogging is how you release your Miniature Schnauzer. For all except the Master Earthdog trials, collars and leads are taken off before the dog enters the test area. You can place your dog on the ground before releasing him, or release him down from a point no higher than waist level. You may not, however, throw your dog toward the den; this kind of stage parenting gets

Scruffts

Once a year, mixed-breed dogs in England can participate in Scruffts, a nationwide competition for crossbreed dogs. If your Miniature Schnauzer is mostly Miniature Schnauzer or just has a bit of Miniature Schnauzer in his background, you can participate.

Dogs compete for the prestigious title of "Scruffts Family Crossbreed Dog of the Year." The cool part is that the competition raises money for dog-related charities, so you will not only have fun but will also be donating to a good cause. What could be better, other than actually winning the competition?

This Mini Schnauzer is making his way through the weave poles, one of several obstacles dogs must negotiate on an agility course.

your Schnauzer kicked out of the test. While releasing the dog, you can give one command without penalty, but then you must be quiet and do nothing until you are instructed to do so by the judge. This is mostly instinctive work, and the dog is supposed to do this on his own.

Earthdog Clubs

Some earthdog club members are terrier and Dachshund owners. These people are a lot of fun, as you would expect from folks who are willing to spend their free time digging a fake tunnel in a specific size and scenting it with a couple of rats.

The goal of the American Working Terrier Association (AWTA) is to encourage owners of terriers and Dachshunds to hunt in the field with their dogs and thus maintain their working abilities. (That's why their logo features three mice, a fox, a squirrel, and a rat.) Miniature Schnauzers are recognized by the AWTA; according to the AWTA, Miniature Schnauzers do an excellent job. No surprise there!

The AWTA grants certificates based on achievement completed. A Certificate of Gameness (CG) is given to qualifying dogs in the

Open Division, and Hunting Certificates (HCs) are granted to dogs who are used to hunt regularly over the course of a year. Working Certificates (WCs) are for dogs who qualify through work in a natural den.

The AKC has specific regulations for earthdog tests. Their noncompetitive program begins with a basic introduction to den work and quarry. The program progresses through gradual steps to require the dog to demonstrate that he is willing to perform the required tasks, including seeking quarry and locating and working it underground.

AGILITY

Dog agility is a competitive sport that tests your training and handling skills over a timed obstacle course. It's the canine equivalent of a horse jumping competition. It debuted in England at the Crufts show in 1978. If you haven't seen an agility competition, you owe it to yourself to at least see this fast-paced, highly motivated festival of physical activity.

Agility has become a hugely popular dog sport, attracting all kinds of breeds and people. It's wonderful exercise for your dog's body and mind and also keeps you from being sedentary. As with obedience competition, training to compete in agility creates a very strong bond between you and your dog because you work so closely together. Miniature Schnauzers are highly suited to the sport. Standard and Giant Schnauzers enjoy it too, but usually aren't as fast as some other breeds in their size categories. Different organizations offer a huge variety of agility titles.

The ultimate obstacle course, agility is as fun for spectators as it is for participants. Dogs jump hurdles, go up and down ramps, race through open and closed tunnels, walk over a see-saw, and weave through a bunch of poles in a straight line. Hours and hours of regular practice and training are involved.

Agility is so popular that many events are televised, but the excitement and enthusiasm of devotees hangs in the air, so attending an event is far, far more exciting than watching a televised one. Spectators get a particular kick out of seeing whether or not a dog follows his handler's instructions. To get the full flavor of agility, it helps to see a live competition.

The AKC, the North American Dog Agility Council (NADAC), and the United States Dog Agility Association (USDAA) all offer

competitive agility trials. The organizing bodies offer different titles. NADAC's Agility Trial Champion is also referred to as NATCH-1 or NATCH-2; their versatility title is Vers-NATCH-1, and so on. The AKC has titles such as Excellent Standard and Excellent Jumpers title, and Master Agility Champion. The USDAA offers such titles as Accomplished Performance Dog, Jumpers Champion, Performance Snooker, Tournament Master, and Veteran Master Agility Dog.

RALLY

For people who are intimidated by the formality of obedience, rally-o (short for obedience) is an excellent choice. It's a lot of fun! Unlike formal obedience, you are allowed to talk to and encourage your dog as much as you want during your run. Food rewards are allowed in the ring.

Rally is a relatively new competitive dog sport in which the dog and handler complete a course designed by the rally judge. The course has 10 to 20 stations, depending on the experience of the handler and dog.

Dog and handler run a course of stations, as in agility, only the moves are mostly like obedience. Weaving is a move learned in agility, and steps like Halt, Sit, and Down are obedience moves. Given that Miniature Schnauzers shine in both obedience and agility, rally is a natural sport for them.

In AKC-sponsored rally-o, the organization not only allows but encourages unlimited communication between handler and dog. The Association of Pet Dog Trainers (APDT) holds rally trials in which all dogs, purebreds and mixed breeds, are welcome.

A sample rally course, as outlined by APDT, may include such moves as:

- HALT—Sit—Down—Walk Around
- Left Turn
- About Turn—Right
- About "U" Turn

- 270-degree Right (Turn)
- 360-degree Right (Turn)
- Call (Dog) Front—Forward Right
- Fast Pace
- Normal Pace
- Moving Side Step Right
- HALT—90-degree Pivot Right—HALT
- Spiral Right—Dog Outside
- HALT—1, 2, 3 Steps Forward
- HALT—Turn Right—1 Step—HALT
- Straight Figure 8
- HALT—Stand—Exam—Leave
- Return & Forward from Stand
- Turn & Call (Dog) Front
- Finish Right
- HALT—180-degree Pivot Left—HALT
- HALT—From Sit—About "U" Turn & Forward
- Call Front—1, 2, 3 Steps Backward
- Send Over Jumps—Handler Runs By
- HALT—Leave—Call (Dog) Front while Running
- Moving Down & Forward
- HALT—Fast Forward from Sit
- HALT—Side Step Right—HALT

FREESTYLE

Both sport and entertainment, freestyle is dog and person dancing to music with choreographed moves. It is simply amazing to watch a dog and person move together like Fred Astaire and Ginger Rogers, using obedience-style moves on the dance floor. If you feel like you don't get to go out dancing enough, canine freestyle is for you. It's good exercise, good fun, and carries an amazing capacity for bonding. It's also a huge crowd-pleaser brought to dog lovers by the World Canine Freestyle Association.

If you haven't seen freestyle done well, understand that it can take your breath away. It's an amazing performance of teamwork by handler and dog. You, the handler, choose the music and design the dance steps. Design the steps with your dog in mind—using what he does best and what he can learn. You can include obedience steps and tricks, anything you can think of. It's excellent exercise for both of you, and a great one-on-one bonding activity.

From a simple request to "dance" on his hind legs, you can develop a whole routine with your dog, set it to music, and compete in canine freestyle.

TRACKING

Using that infamous sense of canine smell that is 10,000 times stronger than a human's, a dog participates in the sport of tracking by following a person's scent trail. Several organizations offer tracking titles.

Many AKC kennel club chapters offer tracking classes, because the AKC offers titles in this sport. Three AKC tracking titles are available: TD, Tracking Dog; TDX, Tracking Dog Excellent or a VST, Variable Surface Tracker; and the highest level of performance—CT, Champion Tracker.

Unlike some other canine sports, in tracking the dog is in charge, not the human. As a sport, tracking is noncompetitive and is always held outdoors, so it is an ideal sport for people who like being outside, bonding with their dog. Your dog has the added benefit of being able to participate alongside Bloodhounds and Basset Hounds for fun.

Tracking is a canine skill with great benefit to humans, because dogs can track game, lost people, police suspects, drugs, pets, and even lost items. While search-and-rescue training and Schutzhund tracking are related in that dogs use their scent ability to track, they require different training than that offered in the AKC training. For example, in search-and-rescue training, the handler helps the dog find the scent, whereas AKC tracking prohibits help from the handler. AKC does not require the defined step-by-step tracking needed for Schutzhund tracking.

FLYBALL

A California invention during the late 1970s, flyball is a fast, fun, social, and motivated sport for dogs who love to run and chase balls. Flyball is a relay race with hurdles. Each team has four dogs. The dogs leave the starting line and jump over four hurdles that are 10 feet (3.0 m) apart to reach a box at the end of the "track." The box is 51 feet (15.5 m) from the starting line.

The dogs step on a spring-loaded device, causing a tennis ball to

shoot out of the box. The dog grabs the tennis ball, turns around, and runs the hurdles again. Just as the first dog crosses the start/finish line, the next dog in the team starts. The first team that has no errors wins the heat. The height of the hurdles is adjusted for the size of the dogs in the team.

Miniature Schnauzers are fast and agile, making them prime contenders in the sport of agility.

According to the North American Flyball Association (NAFA), dogs can earn the following titles:

- FD, Flyball Dog
- FDX, Flyball Dog Excellent
- FDCh, Flyball Dog Champion
- FM, Flyball Master
- FMX, Flyball Master Excellent
- FMCh, Flyball Master Champion
- ONYX, ONYX Award 20000 Plaque
- FGDCh, Flyball Grand Champion
- HOBBES, HOBBES Awards

Contact NAFA at www.flyball.org to find out where flyball classes are held in your area. If your Schnauzer loves to run, jump, and play with balls, he will thank you for it.

CONFORMATION

What does it take to make a conformation show dog? Conformation is what most people think of when they consider dog shows: A lot of fancy, neatly groomed dogs high stepping it around a ring in a sort of canine beauty pageant.

Because not every dog has what it takes, if you want to show in conformation, you must buy a puppy from a responsible breeder, one who shows her own dogs in conformation and has earned championships on several dogs in her line. The dog needs excellent breeding geared for conformation; a Miniature Schnauzer who will do well in the ring will certainly not come from a puppy mill or backyard breeder.

The show Miniature Schnauzer is outgoing, loves the attention and limelight of the ring, has nice manners, is well trained for what he must do while showing, and has the kind of confidence that shouts "Me! Me! I'm the best!" After good breeding, attitude is everything. No wonder the Terrier Group has had more wins at the Westminster Kennel Club than any other group; it's that terrier attitude and sparkle.

Regulations require that your Miniature Schnauzer be registered with the appropriate kennel club in your country, and he cannot be neutered. A Miniature Schnauzer must also have the formal show appearance that involves a stripped or rolled coat—no clippers. Puppies can begin showing at the age of 6 months. No show dog can have disqualifying faults specifically mentioned in the Miniature Schnauzer breed standard.

Showing in the United States and England

In England, the show ring has a more casual atmosphere than does the American ring. Most visitors to British shows find the event to be a relaxed experience. In the Kennel Club, Miniature Schnauzers are in the Utility Group, whereas in the AKC they are in the Terrier Group. Shows in England tend to have a larger number of competitors than they do in the United States.

In England, more dogs are owner-handled than are in the United States. "There are few professional handlers," said Darlene Arden, author of *Unbelievably Good Deals and Great Adventures That You Absolutely Can't Get Unless You're a Dog*. "Also, they wear the dog's number clipped to their clothing, and they wear any ribbons the dog has worn that day. It's more laid back, and people are dressed more casually in the ring."

"There are no 'rings' as such in England," said Chris Walkowicz, an AKC judge and past president of the Dog Writers Association of America. "People sit in chairs around the breed being shown. They will stack the dogs in any direction, as opposed to here, where all dogs face the same way, counter-clockwise.

"Grooming is quite different. Americans really get into hairdressing and plucking stray hairs. The British are more laid back about that, too. They might bathe the dog a week ahead

A top-winning Miniature Schnauzer is a very special dog who represents all that is special in the breed.

or more, bring them from home, and run a brush through at the show. The British are really tough about foreign substances, such as chalk and hairspray, and every now and then they test dogs for foreign substances, so that stuff simply isn't used. Here, we often put it in, then brush it out just before showing," says Walkowicz.

What to Wear When You're Showing

Selecting clothes to wear in the ring is a personal preference, but universally, men and women need pockets in which to put accessible treats. Instead of pockets, you can put the treats in your armband; some women use waistbands, pantyhose, and inside their mouths as storage places for treats (the caveat being that you won't want the really yucky-tasting treats in your mouth, although your Miniature Schnauzer should love them). It's all a matter of preference. If running around makes you warm, you might want to avoid sweaters and heavy clothing.

Handler clothing for conformation tends to be the most formal in the dog world. Not formal as in ball gowns (although you see some handlers coming close to that at the televised Westminster show), but almost businesslike in appearance.

Men should take their cue from the judge, says breeder Jim Discher of PJ's Doghouse in Darlington, Wisconsin. "I think that people showing in conformation should be well dressed, ties and jacket for men, unless it's very hot, in which case you take your clue from the judge. Wear a jacket if the judge wears one, and if the judge has no jacket, I take mine off."

Handlers spend hours with their show dogs, teaching them gaiting patterns and stances to help them show off for the judges.

Women may have special considerations, such as wearing a loose skirt or dress that permits comfortable running. The skirt or dress should be long enough so that you can bend over without thinking about your skirt length but short enough so that it doesn't flap in your dog's face or trip you. You're going to be bending, kneeling, and standing, so practice those movements in outfits you're considering to make sure you stay covered. Pants are fine, and pant suits are seen frequently. A sports bra is a good idea.

"Most women wear dresses or skirts, although in recent years dress slacks have become more popular, especially in the winter," said Pat Discher, also of PJ's Doghouse. "I tend to stay more casual, but that's me. Some handlers dress up in fancier dresses although that's mainly the people who plan on getting into group competitions. I personally like walking shorts. They are comfortable and often come as a coordinated outfit and look good. Pockets are a must in any show outfit."

She also notes that washability is important, and recommends colors that are complementary to the dog. With a solid-colored dog, prints or plaids are okay, as long as they don't overwhelm the dog. With a multicolored dog, solid colors are usually best.

"I have worn black with our black/silver dogs as long as the black does not get behind the dog at any time. For example, I wear black walking shorts with our dogs because when gaiting, the shorts are above the dog. And when the dog is on the table, they are below it, so the shorts are never directly behind the dog when the judge is looking at him," she says.

Color choices are a personal preference. For conformation, most people wear colors that contrast with the dog so that it's easier for the judge to focus full attention on the dog; you should be invisible to the judge, because the dog is the star. In conformation, the Miniature Schnauzer is shown on the table, so the judge doesn't have to lean over. Wear a top color that contrasts with your dog.

"One of the most important things with Miniature Schnauzers is the color," said Jim Discher. "Don't wear anything that will hide the dog. No black with a black dog; I have seen dogs disappear into a black pair of slacks. Remember, the judge sees the dog against the handlers in most cases. I like to wear something that will set off the dog: A red sport coat with a white shirt behind a black and silver dog is a fantastic contrast! You sometimes need to be adventurous." Blue is a popular contrast color; red looks wonderful, but some superstitious people don't use it as much because red indicates second place.

(When dressing for obedience competition, remember that obedience is less formal than conformation competition, and the sporting events are even less formal than that. In obedience, some choose to wear colors that match the dog, to purposely blend in with the dog in the hopes of covering some mistakes. In this case, gray or black pants would be ideal, depending on the color of your Schnauzer.)

Wear shoes in which you can run, since you will be trotting around the ring, too. They don't have to be flat if you can run in them, but this is not a good place to wear open toes, open-heeled shoes, or stiletto heels (no matter how good you look in them).

"This Breed Can Do Anything!"

Schnauzers are quite versatile and can enjoy several canine activities. They participate in earthdog tests, tracking, freestyle, rally, agility, flyball, and more. "I did lure coursing with Sunny a million years ago back in the '80s up in Canada just for fun," said Karen Brittan. "Peter has the first leg of his herding title through the American Herding Breed Association (AHBA) (he used to herd the neighbor's cattle home when they got through our fence), and some Schnauzers do swim, although many hate water. Many Minis have a great herding instinct, thanks to their Standard Schnauzer ancestors. This breed can do absolutely anything."

HEALTH

of Your Miniature Schnauzer

A dog's quality of life can be significantly affected by health issues, for better or worse. It's up to you to take good care of your Mini's health. This entails more than just going in for regularly scheduled checkups; it's knowing what is normal for your Mini and actively looking for potential health concerns throughout your dog's life. It's far easier to treat a disease earlier than later, and staying on top of your Mini Schnauzer's health can make a positive impact.

FINDING A VETERINARIAN

Select a veterinarian before you need one. Finding one during an emergency isn't a good start, and your stress will be significantly less if you have an established relationship with a veterinarian. A good time to do some research about where to go is before your Schnauzer arrives on your doorstep.

The best way to find a good vet is to ask around among your friends and neighbors and see where they go and why they like that particular veterinarian. What do they like about that clinic? Is it one vet they like, or do they like everyone at the clinic? Do they have strong preferences about which vet to see? Also, ask any local veterinary associations, dog clubs, dog schools, or dog groups for recommendations.

From these recommendations, cull through the list by

determining location and hours. If an emergency occurs, the closer you are, the better. That is not to say you should choose based on location, but if you come down to two perfectly good choices, location may make a difference.

Visit the top two clinics on your list and see how the staff interacts with both animals and clients. Tell them on the phone that you are shopping for a new vet. You can get a gut feeling by standing in the lobby and seeing the staff interact with clients. Don't be afraid to ask for an appointment to tour the facility.

Pricing

Because clinics have different approaches to pricing, comparing clinics on price alone is like comparing apples to oranges. One clinic may have a higher fee for a dental exam because they use better anesthesia and monitoring equipment, so don't choose based on price alone. Low prices may mean a lower standard of care, with which you may not be comfortable, or it may mean you end up with a lot of extra fees incurred to make up for a low price designed to get you in the door. It might also mean your vet went to vet school a long time ago, no longer needs to pay back school loans, and is a perfectly fine vet. Just don't let price be your only consideration.

Services

What services are available? Do they have a groomer on staff, or do they board dogs? Is anyone there overnight? Do they have any specialists on staff? Do they have a network of specialists with whom they work on a regular basis?

How does the clinic handle after-hours emergencies, and what do clients do for urgent care? Dogs are notorious for getting sick in the middle of the night or on holidays—will you have to go to an emergency hospital, or will the staff meet you at their clinic? How far away is the emergency hospital they recommend?

Quality of Care

Ask if each dog has a full physical exam prior to every surgery. This added precaution may uncover a previously undetected concern. How early can you drop off your dog for surgery? How late can you pick him up? Ask what safety precautions are taken during surgery—do they put breathing tubes on all anesthetized patients? Do they have a heart and oxygen monitor? Do they have a crash box for cardiac emergencies? Is a fresh sterilized surgical pack used for each surgery?

Ask what safety precautions are taken after surgery. A dog's temperature should be monitored in case he gets too cold, which can negatively affect his heart.

Another significant factor is how they manage pain for their patients. Veterinarians who stay current know how to manage pain; the difference between pain management today and even a decade ago is astounding. Some surgeries, such as orthopedic surgery, are more painful to recuperate from than others, and the ease with which your Miniature Schnauzer recuperates on appropriate pain control is significant. If a veterinarian tells you that animals don't feel pain the way humans do, keep looking. No reason exists for your dog to be in pain after surgery.

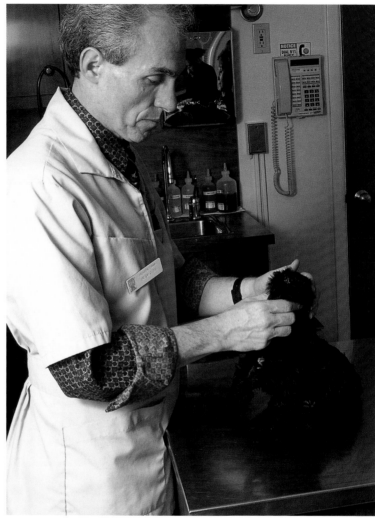

In addition to you and your family, your veterinarian is the person who has the best interest of your dog in mind.

You want to establish a good working relationship with someone you trust. You may be seeing a lot of the clinic, so make sure you're comfortable with it. I see my veterinarian far, far more frequently than I see my physician. If you're interested in alternative medicine or feeding a raw diet, ask how they feel about this, to see if they think it's ineffective or a valuable option. It's best to work with someone who shares your philosophies. Most people choose a veterinarian based on how they feel about the person—it's the personal touch that matters.

That First Visit

Your new dog—whether puppy or adult—should see the veterinarian within 2 days after he arrives in your arms. Bring a fecal sample so your vet can check for worms, which can be quite common and a real nuisance. Schedule a spay/neuter appointment (unless your dog is meant for conformation showing, has already been neutered, or has a medical reason to wait). An overall physical examination should catch any concerns you must take care of.

It is likely that, wherever you got your new dog, he will have already seen a veterinarian. But if this is your puppy's very first vet visit, it's worthwhile to bring the puppy in for nothing more than a get-to-know-you appointment that does not involve shots, toenail clipping, or anything he might not like. Ask the staff to fuss over the puppy (if they haven't started already—anyone who works at a clinic usually loves puppies and kittens). Ask the veterinarian to put your puppy on the exam table, say nice happy things, and give treats without doing anything medical.

It's important that your dog be comfortable at the vet's. This is not wasted money on a visit that isn't needed. Come back within a couple of days for whatever the puppy needs medically, but let that first visit be as positive as possible. Spending over a decade with a dog who despises going to the vet is a huge pain for both of you. That first exposure is critical, so make every effort for it to be a positive one.

PHYSICAL EXAMINATIONS

A physical examination is a hands-on experience for your Miniature Schnauzer. The veterinarian will listen to his heart and lungs; feel his abdomen; examine the skin; check his eyes, ears, and teeth; and look at how he walks and moves. Your dog will also be weighed.

It is amazing how much a veterinarian can find by simply running her hands over a dog and peeking into certain spots. The vet will carefully examine any bumps and lumps; most are benign and no more meaningful than a wart, but some are malignant.

It's a good idea to bring adult dogs in annually for a physical. Senior dogs should probably go in for a physical examination twice yearly. Veterinarians typically run some blood tests on older dogs to check for abnormalities in organ function (kidneys, liver, etc.). Diseases that are discovered in this way usually respond better to treatment.

VACCINATIONS

Recently, vaccination schedules have become a bit controversial. It used to be thought that vaccines couldn't hurt, but now it has been discovered that's not necessarily the case. The "less is more" theory is in vogue when it comes to how often to vaccinate.

The majority of Miniature Schnauzers have no long-term problems with vaccines. However, some researchers believe that overuse of vaccines is related to an increase of autoimmune diseases, and Miniature Schnauzers are known to get autoimmune diseases.

"No one vaccination regimen is appropriate for all dogs," said Linda Sullivan, DVM, a Miniature Schnauzer lover and professor in clinical pathology at the University of Wisconsin School of Veterinary Medicine in Madison, Wisconsin. "Tailor the vaccination protocol to your dog's risks, depending on factors such as geographic location and activities. Having said that, annual vaccinations for most vaccines are unnecessary, and with some vaccines, protection doesn't last a year."

It's a benefit versus risk decision to make, in consultation with your vet, about what's right for you Schnauzer.

Why so Many Puppy Vaccinations?

Puppies are born with their mother's antibodies to protect them against disease. *Antibodies* are an integral part of the body's immune system, which protect your dog from disease. Antibodies are a protein that the body produces in response to foreign invaders called *antigens*. Antibodies render the antigens harmless. Puppies have inexperienced immune systems,

DHLPP and Rabies

The DHLPP booster vaccinations and rabies vaccination that your Miniature Schnauzer receives is for:

- **Distemper,** an airborne viral disease of the lungs and intestines
- **Hepatitis,** a viral disease that affects the liver
- **Leptospirosis,** a bacterial disease spread by infected urine
- **Parainfluenza,** the canine equivalent of infectious bronchitis
- **Parvovirus**, a viral disease affecting the intestines
- **Rabies,** a viral disease of the central nervous system

Vaccinations are necessary to protect puppies and dogs from diseases that could prove fatal.

so your Miniature Schnauzer puppy's immune system must be exposed to or "meet" antigens so that it learns how to produce antibodies to them.

The maternal antibodies don't last very long in a puppy, but when they are active, they negate any vaccinations the puppy receives. The antibodies find the vaccine and kill it, which is exactly what antibodies are supposed to do. You must wait for the mother's antibodies to be gone before a puppy's vaccinations can be effective. Individual antibodies for specific diseases wane at different times, which is why puppies need a series of vaccinations, rather than getting them all at one time.

Vaccination Schedule

Dr. Sullivan agrees with the American Animal Hospital Association's recommendations for vaccination schedules: the puppy series for core vaccines, a booster for adults at 1 year, and boosters every 3 three years thereafter.

The Puppy Series

Puppy shots begin with the DHLPP combination shot and rabies. DHLPP includes distemper, hepatitis, leptospirosis, parainfluenza, and parvovirus. Rabies is a separate shot.

Distemper

Administer one dose at 6 to 8 weeks, 9 to 11 weeks, and 12 to 14 weeks of age.

Hepatitis

Administer one dose at 6 to 8 weeks, 9 to 11 weeks, and 12 to 14 weeks of age.

Leptospirosis

Administer one dose at 6 to 8 weeks, 9 to 11 weeks, and 12 to 14 weeks of age

Parvo

Administer one dose at 6 to 8 weeks, 9 to 11 weeks, and 12 to 14 weeks of age.

Parainfluenza

Administer one dose at 6 to 8 weeks, 9 to 11 weeks, and 12 to 14 weeks of age.

Rabies

Administer one dose as early as 3 months of age.

Optional

Some vaccinations are optional and depend greatly on your geographic location and your dog's lifestyle. Do you live in an urban skyscraper, a suburb, or the woods? Does your Schnauzer participate in earthdog tests, held in rural fields? Does he take agility or obedience lessons on a regular basis, where he comes into contact with other dogs?

Bordetella

If your dog lives in or visits a breeding kennel, shelter, or some other area where multiple dogs are in close contact, then a *bordetella* vaccination is recommended. Most dog schools require that dogs be vaccinated for this before taking a class. *Bordetella* is also known as *kennel cough*. It is a highly contagious respiratory disease similar to a cold. Usually, it goes away on its own, but it is sometimes associated with parainfluenza.

Parainfluenza

Parainfluenza is a highly contagious virus that causes respiratory infections.

Lyme Disease

The Lyme disease vaccination is only recommended if your dog has a high exposure risk, such as living in those areas where deer ticks are common. Deer ticks carry Lyme disease. Your veterinarian can tell you whether your dog is at risk for tick bites.

Giardia

Giardia vaccination is not recommended by most veterinarians, because it does not prevent infection. The internal parasite that causes giardiasis can be passed from pets to people, but most human cases of giardiasis come from human sources, not dogs. *Giardia* is a parasite that dogs can pick up from an affected water source, such as puddles at dog parks or untested well water.

How Healthy Are Miniature Schnauzers?

Most really popular breeds have some genetic health problems. While breed clubs and responsible breeders do their best to eliminate those problems, some still crop up. Miniature Schnauzers are fairly healthy and hearty despite being a very popular breed. They don't need a veterinarian who specializes in them, like some brachycephalic dogs, because the breed doesn't have enough medical oddities.

Titers

Rather than give vaccinations on a calendar schedule, some people like to test for titer levels of the vaccination in their Miniature Schnauzer's blood. Titers are indicators of the quantity of antibodies in the blood for a given disease. If titers are high enough to provide protection, some people choose not to vaccinate their pets. The tests are more expensive than the vaccinations, but some people prefer them to possible unnecessary vaccinations. For most dogs, the core vaccinations tend to be effective for 5 to 8 years, with the exception of leptospirosis, which may wane sooner.

Should I Vaccinate My Dog?

While your veterinarian is a valuable resource and guide, you ultimately decide how often to vaccinate and for what diseases, just as you are responsible for all your dog's medical care.

Some veterinarians suspect that vaccines are causative for autoimmune diseases and cancer in some pets. Cancer that develops as a result of vaccination is called *vaccine-associated sarcoma*. Typically, a tumor develops at the site of injection. It is seen more commonly in cats than in dogs.

On the other hand, vaccination is responsible for ending the epidemic of canine parvovirus, a disease first seen in the 1970s. A common sense, middle-of-the-road approach is probably best. If your dog has autoimmune problems or a significant existing disease, vaccination may not be in your dog's best interest (although the rabies vaccine is required by law). If your dog is otherwise healthy, vaccinating on the AAHA's recommended schedule is a reasonable guide.

COMMON HEALTH ISSUES

Predictability is the hallmark of genetic disease. What differentiates genetic disorders from other diseases is that we can predict *morbidity* (sickness) or *mortality* (death) before any clinical signs are seen, as long as certain diagnostic tests indicate that a given Miniature Schnauzer has a genetic condition.

If your Miniature Schnauzer is diagnosed with a genetically related disease, notify the breeder. The breeder must have this information so that she can work toward eliminating it from the line. Miniature Schnauzers should be tested for any hereditary disease before being bred.

The following are some common health issues seen in Miniature Schnauzers.

Eyes

Grooming your dog provides an excellent opportunity to monitor all parts of his health, including that of his eyes.

Do not buy a Miniature Schnauzer puppy whose parents are not registered with the Canine Eye Registration Foundation (CERF) because Miniature Schnauzers are prone to eye problems.

CERF's goal is to eliminate heritable eye disease in all purebred dogs by forming a centralized national registry. The organization registers those dogs certified to be free of heritable eye disease. The people certifying the dogs are members of the American College of Veterinary Ophthalmologists (ACVO). These veterinary ophthalmologists also collect data on dogs examined by ACVO members to provide information for people concerned with eliminating inheritable eye disease.

After a painless examination of your dog's eyes, the ACVO Diplomate will indicate if any specific disease was found. Breeding advice is offered based on guidelines established for Miniature Schnauzers by the ACVO's genetics committee. CERF and the ACVO are separate organizations that cooperate in

working toward the same goal.

If your dog is found to be free of any eye disease that can be inherited, you (the owner, not your veterinarian) can register him with CERF.

You can look up a potential mate's status before breeding, or you can look up the parents of a puppy in which you're interested. Certification is only valid for 1 year. Thus, owners are encouraged to have their Miniature Schnauzer's eyes checked annually to see if they have developed diseases that occur after dogs reach 1 or 2 years of age, such as cataracts or retinal atrophy.

Cataracts

Congenital (present at birth) cataracts and *microphthalmia* are inherited together as autosomal recessive diseases. (Autosomal diseases are inherited through the non-sex chromosomes; recessive inheritance sometimes causes disease when each parent has an abnormal gene for non-sex chromosomes.) Cataracts are also commonly seen in diabetic dogs, but this type is not congenital. (The dog is not born with any genetic predisposition toward them.)

The lens of the eye focuses light rays, so a cataract impairs vision by blocking light rays. Cataracts don't require treatment; dogs adapt to blindness much better than people do. When they are treated, it's by surgery. Cataract surgery isn't an option unless a determination is made that it can restore vision. (If the retina is also diseased, then vision cannot be restored.)

If your dog has cataracts and is a candidate for surgery, a veterinary ophthalmologist should perform the outpatient procedure. The lens capsule is removed, the lens is broken up with ultrasonic waves, and the cataract particles are drawn out. Afterward, the lens can be replaced with an artificial lens that allows sharper vision. (Inserting a new lens is an expensive option that can be done at your request.) Sometimes the lens cannot be replaced, depending on which stage the cataract is in.

Lens replacement is not essential; although most dogs see much better with the artificial lens, dogs still see better without the bad lens than they did with it. Without a lens implant, your dog will see objects in reverse, as though he is looking in a mirror, but he will still be able to see.

A small cataract will grow into a large one over time. Today, veterinary ophthalmologists prefer to remove cataracts when they're still small and soft. Years ago, surgery was delayed until the dog was blind. The prognosis for dogs with diabetic or inherited cataracts is very good.

Microphthalmia

Microphthalmia is a birth defect in which one or both eyes are smaller than normal. This means that the field of vision is restricted. By itself, this condition is not a problem, but it is sometimes associated with more severe eye defects such as retinal dysplasia and cataracts. No diagnostic tests or treatments are available, although the eye can be enucleated (removed) if it causes discomfort. It is unlikely to cause such discomfort unless other problems also affect the eye.

Entropion

Eyelids are meant to protect the eyes, so a malformation can cause the opposite effect. *Entropion* is a condition in which the eyelids turn inward so that the eyelashes rub against the cornea (the transparent layer over the front of the eye). The ongoing irritation can result in corneal ulcers or scarring of the cornea surface. Sometimes only the lower lid is affected, but often both lids are involved.

The condition is diagnosed through an ocular examination and must be recognized early to prevent damage to the cornea. The usual treatment is surgery to remove the extra skin and muscle from the eyelid. Ophthalmic ointment can soften the eyelashes so that they aren't as abrasive to the cornea.

Some pups with congenital entropion eventually grow out of it as they mature, so surgery usually isn't done until about 6 months of age. In puppies, temporary tacking sutures can pull the lids out away from the surface long enough to determine if corrective surgery is warranted.

It's best to have a surgeon experienced in this condition do the surgery. Overcorrecting can be a serious problem. The eyelid may then roll too much in the other direction, or the dog may not be able to close his eye all the way. Either of these complications can irritate the cornea and may require either further surgery or a lifetime of eye medications.

The genetic tendency toward entropion is not defined and vision is not destroyed, so dogs with entropion can still get a CERF number. Entropion tends not to be as severe in Miniature Schnauzers as it is in breeds such as Mastiffs, Bullmastiffs, Sharpeis, and Chow Chows, where heavily wrinkled facial skin affects the eyes.

Progressive Retinal Atrophy (PRA)

Progressive retinal atrophy is not one specific disease; rather, it encompasses a group of hereditary retinal diseases. The retina is the part of the eye that senses light. PRA shows up well after a dog passes into adulthood and normally isn't seen in Miniature Schnauzers until they're about 3 years old.

Almost all forms of PRA lead to blindness. Night blindness is commonly the first sign in most forms. PRA is diagnosed by an ophthalmic exam. No treatment is available, nor is there any way to stop the disease from progressing.

PRA is inherited through an autosomal recessive gene that can occur in Miniature Schnauzers as well as Schnauzer mixes. Two recessive genes are needed to produce a dog with PRA, one from each of a puppy's parents, so it's very difficult to remove PRA from a breed, much less from a line. Only buy a puppy who has been bred from dogs who are certified free of PRA, so that your dog will have less risk of developing it. Your Miniature Schnauzer could develop it anyway, but hedge your bets by asking to see the CERF registrations from both parents.

Miniature Schnauzers as a breed are prone to eye problems. Talk to your dog's breeder about any testing that's been done in your dog's line.

Miniature Schnauzers who have PRA should not be bred. They should be spayed or neutered rather than risk passing on blindness. A DNA test is available for Miniature Schnauzers to look for Type A PRA. (This is not the case with all breeds.) However, the jury is still out on whether this is truly needed or even helpful. The

Eye Committee of the American Miniature Schnauzer Club does not favor mandatory DNA testing for PRA at this time.

Calcium Oxalate Urolithiasis (Urinary Stones)

While a genetic connection is not scientifically proven, Miniature Schnauzers are predisposed to forming calcium oxalate stones in the urinary tract. A common mineral compound, calcium oxalate appears as crystals in urine. About three-quarters of affected dogs are male. The stones form when changes in metabolic factors cause *hypercalciuria*, or excessive calcium in the urine.

If your dog has bloody urine, pees frequently, and strains to urinate, get him checked for urinary stones, which can be in any part of his urinary system. Because these signs can be caused by other conditions, the veterinarian will try to detect stones by palpating (a fancy term for feeling and squishing his belly) your dog's abdomen, and if necessary, taking X rays and/or an ultrasound.

Treatment depends on where the stones are located, especially if they are blocking urine flow. Very small stones can be flushed out during an office visit, but larger stones usually require surgery.

Getting rid of stones doesn't mean you can stop worrying about them. Stones usually recur, typically in about 3 years. Although dietary changes cannot dissolve existing stones, they can help prevent new ones from forming, and your veterinarian will most likely suggest a prescription diet as well as an increase in water intake.

Dogs may also be given potassium citrate to create a more inhospitable atmosphere for stone formation. Some dogs with stones benefit from taking certain diuretics.

If your dog has been treated for stones, he should have frequent urinalyses.

Comedone Syndrome (Schnauzer Bumps)

Again, while no scientifically proven genetic connection exists, Miniature Schnauzers are prone to comedones, dilated hair follicles filled with sebaceous material and skin cells, on their backs. Comedone syndrome is a keratinization—a hardening and drying out—problem of hair follicles along the back. Occasionally, hair loss (alopecia) is also seen with it.

Minis are so prone to the syndrome that it is often referred to as

Your Responsibility

Your vet is not the only person responsible for the health and well-being of your Miniature Schnauzer—you are as well. You are responsible for feeding quality, nutritious food, visiting the veterinarian when necessary, grooming so that his coat doesn't mat and cause skin irritation, maintaining a healthy weight, and exercising him enough. His mental stimulation is mostly up to you because a Miniature Schnauzer left to snooze on the couch all day won't be as bright and robust as he would be with lots of exercise, activity, and stimulation. Your vet can't keep your dog healthy without your cooperation. You are your dog's first line of defense, part of a team working toward keeping your dog healthy.

Schnauzer Bumps or Schnauzer comedone syndrome. Miniatures are more likely to have it than are Standard or Giant Schnauzers.

If your dog has it, he will likely have it for life, because it is a chronic condition with no cure. The best you can do is provide good care. Benzoyl peroxide or alcohol wipes can help reduce the incidence of bumps. Medicated shampoos or gels containing benzoyl peroxide can be effective as well. Supplementing your Schnauzer's diet with vitamin A can help, too.

Congenital Megaesophagus

The word *megaesophagus* means "large esophagus." The esophagus is the tube leading from the throat to the stomach. In the megaesophagus, food and liquid accumulate and are retained in the dog's esophagus, which causes him to regurgitate, or "spit up" his food. Regurgitation is not vomiting, because only undigested food and liquid stuck in the esophagus are brought up, not food from the stomach.

The disease is diagnosed with a physical exam, and as needed, blood tests, urinalysis, X rays, and endoscopy. Thyroid function should be checked.

Miniature Schnauzers afflicted with bumps on their back benefit from baths with soothing shampoos.

Most Miniature Schnauzers can be treated at home unless they get aspiration pneumonia or their esophagus becomes obstructed, including with foreign bodies, in which case surgery may be needed. Medications are not available to treat the megaesophagus itself, only any associated conditions, like pneumonia, which may arise.

Diets can be modified to produce the least amount of regurgitation. When modifying the diet, see if your dog does better on liquid or solid foods.

Because every individual is different, you may have to experiment for a while. It's helpful to train your Miniature Schnauzer to eat while standing up; your dog should also stand upright for 10 to 15 minutes after eating. If necessary, feeding tubes can be used. Nausea medications can provide comfort, and antacids can help minimize potential damage to the dog's esophagus when the food is regurgitated.

The prognosis for any dog with megaesophagus is unfortunately poor, whether the dog is treated or not, although congenital megaesophagus occasionally resolves as the puppy ages.

Megaesophagus is not commonly seen in Miniature Schnauzers, but the breed is predisposed to this autosomal dominant inherited condition.

Hereditary X-Linked Muscular Dystrophy (Myotonia Congenita)

This progressive, inherited disease is similar to human muscular dystrophy. Muscle growth is too rapid, and muscles are weak and do not function normally. When an affected dog stops walking, the muscles he used keep moving. (This delay in relaxation does not cause muscle cramping or pain.)

Levels of the enzyme creatine kinase (CK), which is associated with muscle injury and inflammation, become elevated, as does the enzyme lactate dehydrogenase (LDH). Affected dogs have a stiff gait that improves with exercise, although some dogs with muscular dystrophy are exercise intolerant. The disease affects skeletal as well as heart muscle.

Diagnostics involve a medical history, blood tests, and an electromyogram (EMG) to see how well muscles function. The drug *procainamide* helps some dogs. Unfortunately, the heart failure and pneumonia associated with this disease are often fatal.

The gene for this disease is carried by females, but only males get it (sex-linked). It is seen mostly in puppies and young dogs; it has been noticed in puppies as young as 6 weeks. Miniature Schnauzers should be tested for muscular dystrophy before being bred.

Persistent Müllerian Duct

This inherited autosomal recessive trait is quite complex, but it boils down to a fairly simple consequence: A male Miniature Schnauzer can be born with both male and female sexual organs.

An affected dog must be both neutered *and* spayed, because the dog has a uterus and cervix, oviducts, and part of the vagina as well as testicles and sometimes a penis. The dogs appear masculine in all respects.

Typically, this condition is not found on a regular physical examination, but is discovered when the dog has signs of either a uterine infection (pyometra), a urinary tract infection (to which Miniature Schnauzers are prone), or a prostate infection.

Although the dog with this condition is fertile, it certainly should not be bred. While the testes usually develop normally, it is quite common for such a dog to be *cryptorchid*, which means that one or both testicles do not descend. Cryptorchidism is also inherited as a sex-limited autosomal recessive trait. Technically, only the female sexual parts could be removed, but complete sterilization is best, not only to prevented an unwanted breeding, but also for the dog's general health.

Keep an eye on your Mini Schnauzer, even when you think he's safely contained; any number of things could happen to potentially hurt him.

Bleeding Disorders

Miniature Schnauzers are genetically proven to be likely to inherit either one of two bleeding disorders: von Willebrand's disease or Factor VII deficiency.

Von Willebrand's occurs occasionally in the breed, but Factor VII deficiency is rare. Both of these diseases are usually experienced as a tendency toward bleeding, rather than the severe, spontaneous hemorrhage seen in hemophilia. Neither von Willebrand's disease or Factor VII deficiency is as hard on the patient as is hemophilia. All in all, these bleeding disorders are rare within the breed.

Dogs who have been diagnosed with diabetes can still live normal lives with the proper diet, exercise, and medication.

Dogs with von Willebrand's disease are missing a substance that helps platelets form blood clots and that stabilizes Factor VIII during clotting. The substance has been named *von Willebrand's factor*. Because the blood doesn't clot in a timely fashion, dogs with this disease bleed more than normal when they are injured or have surgery. The dogs may also get nosebleeds, and their gums might bleed. If bleeding occurs in the stomach, the feces or urine may contain blood. Blood can leak into the joints, causing symptoms similar to arthritis.

A blood test is given to make the diagnosis. Treatment consists of blood transfusions and injury prevention. No cure is possible. Affected Miniature Schnauzers should not be bred, even though the disease is considered to be a mild to moderate disorder.

Factor VII deficiency is rare but mild. It is not typically associated with spontaneous bleeding, but dogs may bruise easily or have prolonged bleeding after surgery. Factor VII is diagnosed using blood work, and it is treated with plasma transfusion.

Other Conditions to Which Schnauzers Are Prone

Just because no genetic connection exists doesn't mean your Miniature Schnauzer won't develop a disorder not mentioned here. Any dog can develop diabetes, heart disease, kidney troubles, or other conditions. Take good care of your Miniature Schnauzer by feeding him a quality diet, providing plenty of exercise, and not letting him become overweight. Protect him from injury, and you'll be in the best shape to deal with any medical problems that come his way.

Some breed resources mention that Miniature Schnauzers are prone to several diseases for which no scientific proof of heredity exists. It may be entirely possible that no genetic connection exists, or it may be entirely possible that a genetic connection is present, but medical science has not yet been able to establish it.

Interviewing different breeders about Mini health issues results in varying opinions, because different lines are affected by different conditions. Certainly, it would be an extremely rare Miniature Schnauzer who had more than a few of the conditions mentioned.

Diabetes Mellitus

Dogs can have diabetes too. People have either Type 1, which is lack of insulin, or Type 2, which means the pancreas produces insulin, but cells in the body become resistant to it. Type 2, also called adult onset, is most common in people. Dogs get Type 1, or insulin-dependent diabetes. The mean age of onset in dogs is 9 years. Untreated dogs won't live more than a few months unless treatment begins.

In a non-diabetic dog, the pancreas produces the hormone *insulin* in response to elevations in blood glucose, as occur following a meal. Insulin helps a dog use or store the glucose, or sugar, he gets from food.

Weight loss occurs in untreated diabetics because, when there isn't enough insulin, the glucose isn't available as an energy source for muscles. Diabetic dogs have elevated blood glucose levels. The dog urinates more often and drinks a lot more water to keep up with the excessive urine output. That's why the most common signs of diabetes in dogs are increased water consumption and urination, also called *polydipsia* and *polyuria*. Other signs are increased appetite and weakness, vomiting, lethargy, kidney failure, possibly coma, and death.

Dogs are treated with insulin injections, dietary modifications, and exercise. Because dogs can't take insulin in pill form because it breaks down during digestion, it must be injected into the fat underneath the skin to get into the bloodstream. Only human-grade insulin is available, so dog owners must purchase insulin and syringes from a regular pharmacy.

The dicey part of treatment for diabetes in dogs comes in the very early stages. Determining the appropriate dose of insulin can be tricky, but once it's established, maintenance is easier.

The truly critical part of treating diabetes in dogs is consistency: They need the same amount of food and exercise every day. A quality diet that is high in fiber, low in fat, and high in complex carbohydrates is best.

Owners must be on the lookout for diabetic-related cataracts and signs of vision troubles. Diabetes is a frightening diagnosis, but diabetic dogs can have a good quality of life with proper care.

Hypothyroidism

The most common hormone imbalance in dogs, hypothyroidism occurs when a dog doesn't produce enough thyroid hormone and his metabolism is affected. Almost every cell in a dog's body can be affected when thyroid levels are reduced. When a dog has hypothyroidism, he can show signs in several different parts of the body, including the heart, central nervous system, and eyes.

The condition may have several causes, including immune-mediated destruction or natural atrophy of the thyroid or iodine deficiency in the diet, or it may occur as a congenital problem. Immune-mediated destruction and natural atrophy of the thyroid are most common. Generally speaking, it affects middle-aged or older dogs.

Most hypothyroid dogs have some kind of skin problems. If your Miniature Schnauzer has chronic skin problems, have his thyroid function checked. Some dogs have hair loss, and a few have dry coats. About half of affected dogs are obese and lethargic, and some are anemic.

Blood tests are diagnostic. Usually, your veterinarian will perform the Baseline T3 and T4 (thyroid hormones) tests as well as the Thyroid Stimulating Hormone (TSH) test.

Once the thyroid function is reduced, the condition must be treated for life. Untreated, male dogs become sterile and females have infertility issues. Both sexes will have very little hair, feature black pigment on the skin, and will be lethargic. They can become anemic, and heart rates can slow down. Small dogs with hypothyroidism might develop megaesophagus and laryngeal paralysis. Thyroid levels are connected to other diseases, so if another disease is present, complications may increase.

Thankfully, hypothyroidism is easily treated with an inexpensive pill. Treatment of adult onset disease is quite successful; however, *congenital hypothyroidism*, a condition with which puppies are born, causes an abnormal growth rate, and most affected puppies do not survive to adulthood.

Pancreatitis

Pancreatitis is inflammation of the pancreas. Acute pancreatitis is a rapid onset of the inflammation, and this can be fatal. The pancreas has two major functions. It helps metabolize sugar (glucose) by producing insulin, and it helps digest nutrients by producing pancreatic enzymes.

Occasionally, medications a dog is taking for other conditions or a metabolic disorder can cause pancreatitis. Dogs who eat a diet high in fat—most particularly those who are prone to stealing from the garbage or eating fatty table scraps—tend to have pancreatitis more than dogs who don't. Food binges are often the cause of acute pancreatitis.

Dogs with pancreatitis typically have a hunched-up posture caused by the pain in their abdomen, which is distended. Other symptoms include loss of appetite, fever, depression, and dehydration. Vomiting typically occurs, as does diarrhea with a yellowish stool. Blood tests detect increased levels of the pancreatic enzymes *amylase* and *lipase* in affected dogs.

There's no escaping the parasites that may prey on your Mini Schnauzer in the great outdoors, so be prepared with preventive measures.

Acute cases usually call for hospitalization. Treatment involves giving the pancreas a break by not eating, drinking, or taking meds for 24 hours. Fluids are provided intravenously. Dogs who experience significant pain are given pain relievers. If the cause is determined to be a specific medication, that medication is stopped. If the attack was caused by an underlying condition, that condition is treated.

Often unpredictable, pancreatitis can be a lifelong problem, or it

What to Do if Your Dog Is Lost

The best steps to take to find a lost dog are taken before he is lost. First, your dog should wear a collar and identification (ID) tags. Many show dogs don't wear collars because they can rub and damage the coat at the neck; however, if your dog is not a show dog, he should not leave the house without wearing a collar and tags. Some people choose to keep their dogs' tags on at all times, but dogs have been known to accidentally harm each other by pulling on the collar during play. Do what makes sense in your situation.

The ID tag should list, at a minimum, your dog's name and your phone number. Gina Spadafori, author of the nationally syndicated column "Pet Connection," believes that the most important information you can place on a tag is REWARD, because she finds that people are more willing to put effort into getting your dog back to you quickly if there's a little something in it for them. Spadafori recommends listing both your phone number and that of a friend or relative. Spadafori is a big proponent of what she calls the "Annual Neck Check" on New Year's Day, in which you check the status and wear of the collar and legibility of the tags, and replace them if worn.

Get a microchip into your dog. (For more information, see Chapter 3.) My dogs didn't mind being microchipped, and I feel much safer knowing they are. An ID tag and microchip should be used in tandem to complement each other—one is not enough. An identifying tattoo is a third option.

If, despite your best intentions, your dog becomes lost, first, call all local shelters and give them a description of your dog. Then, take in a flyer with his picture. Next, put up signs around the neighborhood as you drive around looking for him. If he is missing long enough, put an ad in the lost and found section of the newspaper.

may only occur once. If a dog has just one episode, limiting fats in the diet may be all that's necessary to prevent another case. If the condition becomes chronic, the severity of the episodes tends to increase. Dogs with either chronic or acute pancreatitis can recover, but it is also possible to die from complications.

The risk of contracting pancreatitis increases for dogs who have other metabolic concerns such as diabetes, hyperadrenocorticism (overproduction of adrenalin), or hypothyroidism, or who have epilepsy or gastrointestinal tract disease.

If a dog gets chronic pancreatitis, diabetes or *pancreatic insufficiency* can result. In pancreatic insufficiency, the dog cannot metabolize nutrients, which pass out of the body undigested. Such a dog has an unremitting appetite, diarrhea, and weight loss, and can even starve to death despite eating enormous amounts of food. Enzyme supplements and diet modification are used to treat pancreatic insufficiency.

PARASITES

All kinds of parasites can plague your dog, including roundworms, hookworms, fleas, ticks, tapeworms, ear mites, and more. Talk about disgusting! Parasites negatively impact your dog's health. In all cases, the sooner the parasites are eliminated— or prevented—the better off your dog will be.

Fleas

Fleas are blood suckers. They carry disease, cause discomfort and allergies, and are generally annoying because their bites itch. Fond of a wide variety of mammalian hosts, fleas jump up to bite a host; they don't fly. Fleas were the bane of a dog's existence before really effective topical controls hit the market.

Adult females lay eggs right on a dog host. Those eggs fall off and hatch where they land. (That's why they infest carpeting.) Larvae eventually hatch, and these larvae feed on organic material before developing into the pupal stage. Pupae may lay dormant for a long time, but they can develop into adult fleas immediately. The resulting adult fleas look for a host from which to suck blood. After

If a flea infestation is suspected, you must clean every surface with which your Mini Schnauzer comes into contact.

feeding, the females lay their eggs, and the cycle starts all over again.

Dogs with any level of flea hypersensitivity scratch at flea bites and irritate the skin even more than the flea did. Sometimes hair loss occurs, or the skin below the hair looks red and irritated.

The only way to get rid of fleas is to break their life cycle. Select a product that indicates on the label that it is an insect growth regulator because, if you only kill the adult fleas, you're getting rid of only about 5 percent of the problem. The most effective first step is to use a topical adulticide, such as fipronil or selamectin.

Another first step is a systemic drug called lufenuron. These medications are available by prescription only, and you can get them at your vet's. These either keep fleas off your dog or kill fleas when they bite. Unless your veterinarian directs you otherwise, only use one of these products at a time.

Some breeds are overly sensitive to these medications, but the Miniature Schnauzer is not one of them. Your veterinarian will also guide you in your selection of products that are best for your Miniature Schnauzer; some products have age minimums or cannot be used in pregnant or nursing dogs. Caution should be used in the selection of flea preventives on sick, immune-compromised, or underweight dogs. Some wash off easily, while some don't. Many products combat more than one type of parasite at a time, including heartworms, fleas, and ticks.

The over-the-counter flea remedies found in pet supply stores use weaker chemicals, which may not be as effective as those provided through a veterinarian.

It also important to clean up the environment where your dog spends his time, both indoors and out. Treat appropriate areas in the house. You can do this yourself or hire a professional exterminator, which you may need if the infestation is very bad.

Vacuum frequently. Wash dog bedding in hot water, and if you have an infestation, replace your dog's bed. Mop hard floors. You must treat your yard as well—a variety of powders, sprays, and microscopic parasitic nematodes are available.

If your Schnauzer regularly snuggles up or sleeps with your cat, she may also need to be treated for fleas, but be sure to get a cat product from your vet for this. Never use any canine flea control products on your cat. Cats have very different and comparatively sensitive systems, and using products labeled for dogs can kill them, even those products using permethrin (an organic material from chrysanthemums), and even when adjusted for weight. Many calls to the National Animal Poison Control Center originate because dog products were used on cats.

Ticks

Ticks are skin parasites. Like spiders and mites, ticks are arthropods that suck blood from their hosts (as opposed to fleas, which are insects that suck blood). As with fleas, ticks can transmit diseases when they suck blood, including Lyme disease, ehrlichiosis, babesiosis, and Rocky Mountain spotted fever.

Lyme disease, which causes recurrent arthritis and lameness, is easier to treat in dogs than in people, but it still takes a long time, and it's not a piece of cake. Ehrlichiosis can

Puppies can have worms passed to them through their mother's milk. This condition is not serious and is easily remedied with medication.

Avian Tuberculosis

Why is there mention of bird tuberculosis when discussing Miniature Schnauzer health? *Mycobacterium avium (M. avium)* has been found in a handful of Miniature Schnauzers in recent years. Affected dogs have signs similar to lymphoma. *M. avium* is an opportunistic disease, which means that dogs or people don't normally get it unless an immune-system problem or a genetic defect is already present. The scientific evidence that Miniature Schnauzers are genetically predisposed to *M. avium* is circumstantial at this point, although that could change. Enough cases have been reported however, including littermates, for some Miniature Schnauzer fanciers to be concerned. At this point, the incidence is quite rare, but it is always best to be aware.

cause inflammation and organ damage, and it harms bone marrow activity. Babesiosis causes red blood cell destruction and anemia. Rocky Mountain spotted fever can cause heart inflammation, internal hemorrhage, and organ failure.

Ticks are very annoying, but don't get so ticked off that you can't act to prevent ticks or the diseases they carry. Many products help prevent ticks from attaching to your Schnauzer and doing their vampire thing, and the products best suited for him depend on your geographic area and the age of your dog. Some of these products can be used on puppies. Never use more than one preventive product at a time.

Avoid walking in the woods during prime flea and tick season, usually during warm weather. It also helps to keep the grass and weeds in your yard mowed short. Spray-on insecticides or repellants intended for use on clothing or humans should never be used on pets.

Ticks do not jump or fly; they crawl or drop down onto their hosts. They are attracted to motion, light patterns, warmth, and carbon dioxide (the stuff you exhale). They tend to climb onto tall objects like fences or high vegetation and wait for a mammal to walk by. Because the blood suckers are attracted to motion, they crawl or climb on you when you walk by in the woods.

Tick bites don't hurt, and most people don't even notice when a tick bites them, much less their dog. I don't know how many times I've found ticks on the top of my head. However, a bite can become infected, and your dog may need oral antibiotics if a lesion occurs.

If you find a tick on your dog, remove it as soon as you can, because if it's taken off within 48 hours, you can prevent disease transmission. For safety's sake, dab rubbing alcohol on the tick, use tweezers to grab it, and pull on the tick slowly and steadily. Be sure not to leave the head embedded. When you have removed the tick, make sure that it's dead—they've been known to survive being tossed down the toilet or sink, and come back for another bite. Drop the removed tick into alcohol or insecticide to make sure you have killed it.

Worms

While dogs can get several types of worms, the four they most commonly get are roundworms, tapeworms, hookworms, and whipworms.

Dogs who travel often and who visit places where other dogs frequent are more likely to pick up worms from other dogs.

Roundworms

Two species of roundworms infect dogs: *Toxocara canis* and *Toxascaris leonina*. Intellectually speaking, *Toxocara canis* has a fascinating life cycle involving travel. Eggs are passed from the host in the host's feces. Eggs containing second-stage larva are picked up by your dog when he eats something containing these eggs, and the eggs hatch in his intestinal tract.

The baby worm burrows out of the intestinal tract and into other body tissues. These second-stage larvae may stay in body tissues for a long time, even years. In dogs, the larvae tend to reside in the liver.

Eventually, it's time to move along, and the larvae pass into the dog's lungs, where they develop into third-stage larvae. Serious pneumonia can result from this invasion. When they move from the lung to the upper airways, they cause the dog to cough. When the dog coughs, he passes the third-

stage larvae into his throat, swallows it, and it goes right back to his intestines.

However, if your Miniature Schnauzer is pregnant, the second-stage larvae do not move to the lung, but to the uterus and the unborn puppies. They develop into third-stage larvae in the puppies' lungs instead of in the mother's lungs.

Once the third-stage larvae are back in the intestine, they mature into fourth-stage larvae and mate. The first eggs are laid about 1 week after the fourth stage larvae have arrived in the intestine. The cycle repeats; the whole cycle only takes about 4 or 5 weeks after infection has first occurred.

The dog may not show any signs, so you may not suspect roundworms, which is why many veterinarians recommend regular deworming. However, if your dog (particularly a puppy) vomits a long, white worm, it's likely a roundworm. These worms can be up to 7 inches (17.8 cm) in length.

Understand that killing off a migrating worm can take some time. When you deworm adult dogs, the only worms that are killed are those in the intestine, which accounts for only part of the life cycle. Once you've cleared out worms from the intestine, new migrating worms return to the intestines. Therefore, an infected dog should be dewormed three or four times.

The other worm, *Toxascaris leonina*, isn't a traveling man. These guys do not migrate through the body. Their second-stage larva matures in the intestine, which takes about 2 to 3 months. Because they stay in the intestine, it's easier to get rid of them.

Toxocara canis can affect people, too. Children occasionally get the worm from playing outside in contaminated soil and putting their fingers in their mouths. Despite not being in the species-appropriate host, the dog roundworm tries its best to complete its life cycle anyway. While traveling in the human, it gets stuck somewhere, usually the eye, creating a huge inflammatory reaction. If the worm dies while in a human eye, blindness typically results.

Tapeworms

The adult *Dipylidium caninum* lives in a dog's small intestine. It clamps onto a dog's intestinal wall with a hook-like appendage, and also uses six rows of teeth to stay attached. Although the whole adult tapeworm is about 6 inches (15.2 cm) long or longer, people only notice small portions of it. These individual segments are white, flat, and look like rice.

Once attached to the intestinal wall, the tapeworm grows a long tail. It has several tail segments. Each tail segment has an independent digestive system and reproductive tract (oh joy). The tapeworm absorbs nutrients through its skin as digesting food flows by. Older tail segments move toward the tip of the tail as new tail segments are formed.

By the time a segment gets to the tip of the worm's tail, the only part of it that remains is the reproductive tract, so when it drops off, it's like dropping a bag full of tapeworm eggs. That little bag, about the size of one grain of rice, is then passed out of the dog's body with his feces. The dropped bag breaks open, spreading tapeworm eggs like an avalanche.

A most amusing and ironic occurrence at this point is that larval fleas, who apparently are not gourmet in nature, eat tapeworm eggs. (Don't you love the idea of parasites eating each other?) However, as the larval flea grows, so does the tapeworm. While the flea sucks blood, it is sometimes licked up and thus ingested by its host, your dog—so much for that free lunch.

The dead flea's body is reduced by normal digestive processes, but the smart little tapeworm is released, finds a nice spot on your dog's intestinal wall to hang onto, and the whole cycle begins again.

The only way your Schnauzer can get tapeworms is from eating fleas, including those on rodents they kill and ingest. The obvious prevention for tapeworms is to control the flea population. Treatment involves a specific drug for deworming (not the same as used to treat other worms) that your veterinarian can provide. Technically, only one deworming treatment is needed, but many veterinarians recommend a second treatment 3 weeks later to be thorough.

Hookworms

Like fleas and ticks, hookworms suck blood, but they can suck significant amounts. Most worms absorb digested food through their skin as the food floats by in the intestines (that's why they are parasites), but adult hookworms clamp down six, sharp, hook-like teeth onto an intestinal wall and drink blood. They mate and live out the rest of their lives in the intestine, and

Alternative remedies are more and more accessible and successful in helping to treat a variety of problems in Miniature Schnauzers and other animals.

are passed out with the feces. They can be transmitted to unborn puppies as well as to people.

The female adult lays eggs in a dog's small intestine. Those eggs are passed into the dog's feces and move out of the body. If the eggs find a nice, warm, moist environment, they develop into larvae within a week. Larvae enter a dog through the skin or mouth. After getting into the body, the hookworm can migrate around for a bit or go directly to the small intestines, where they mature into adults and lay eggs. It's hard to get rid of hookworms if both eggs and larvae are in the small intestine.

Some dogs show no signs of having hookworms; others may have a life-threatening level of blood loss. If the latter occurs, the dog may have pale gums and tongue, tarry feces, either diarrhea or constipation, and even sudden death occurring from blood loss. Puppies are more likely to die from blood loss than are adult dogs, especially if they are also losing blood to fleas.

Your veterinarian will select the appropriate deworming medication. You can stop pregnant mothers from passing hookworms to unborn puppies with daily deworming done under a veterinarian's care.

Whipworms

The whipworm that affects dogs, *Trichuris vulpes*, is smaller than other worms, only about a $1/2$ half inch (1.3 cm) long. Dogs get them from eating whipworm eggs in a contaminated environment. Whipworms can live in soil for years, and it is almost impossible to eradicate whipworms from contaminated ground.

What looks like the whipworm's head is technically the

digestive end, which is skinny. The fat end is the reproductive end. The skinny and fat ends result in a whip-like shape.

Evidence of the worm is hardly ever seen because it lives in the cecum—the point at which the large intestine meets the small intestine. The adult worms bite tissue in the intestine to suck blood. Whipworms lay eggs in the large intestine, and those eggs pass with feces.

A few whipworms generally aren't a problem, but a significant infestation of whipworms can cause bloody diarrhea in dogs because the large intestine becomes inflamed. There isn't enough blood loss to be a problem by itself, but the diarrhea can become chronic and difficult to control. This is not a problem in a healthy dog, but can be a concern for a dog with a compromised immune system.

Diagnosis is made with a fecal examination. An affected dog can be dewormed with specific medication from the veterinarian; some of the medications used to treat other types of worms may not work on whipworms. Repeated treatments are often necessary after 1 or 2 months because of the worm's long maturation cycle, during which time the dog should have periodic fecal exams to make certain reinfection has not occurred. Humans and pet cats cannot become infected with the dog variety of whipworm.

Compounding Pharmacies

As your dog's owner, your compliance in giving medication to your dog as prescribed is important, but the other part of the equation is how compliant your dog is about taking the offered medication. Your Schnauzer is less likely to accept his medicine if it smells like formaldehyde rather than if it tastes and smells like a liver treat. If your dog must take medicine over a long period, and he fights you every time you administer it, a compounding pharmacy may help make his meds more acceptable to him.

These pharmacies can compound your dog's medication into something more palatable that he will be willing to take. Usually, medications end up with chicken, beef, peanut butter, salmon, tuna, or liver flavors. These flavors can be used in capsules, liquids, tablets, and chews. Thus, medicating becomes a treat rather than a battle, and you and your dog will both be much happier at medicine time.

Compounding pharmacies are ideal for long-term needs. They can also customize dosages so that you don't have to cut pills in half, and you can select which format (chews or liquid, for example) that you think your dog will tolerate best. You can also switch flavor or form to alleviate potential boredom with his compound over time.

SPAYING AND NEUTERING FOR HEALTH

Altering (surgical sterilization to prevent reproduction) is not only good for your Miniature Schnauzer's long-term health, it can lessen some behavioral problems associated with reproductive hormones. Unless you plan to breed your healthy, happy, registered Miniature Schnauzer, it's best for the dog's health that he be altered.

The age at which it is safe and appropriate to alter is younger than it used to be years ago. Veterinarians now recommend that altering any time after 8 to 10 weeks of age is fine if the animal is healthy.

Females

Removing both ovaries and the uterus is called a spay. It is major surgery but very common. Spaying prevents a female from being able to come into *heat*—the time when a dog is able to mate—and become pregnant.

If spayed before her first heat, a bitch (fertile female) has almost zero possibility of developing mammary cancer. If the surgery is done after her first heat, she has a 7 percent chance of developing it. If the surgery is done after her second heat, she has a one-in-four chance (25 percent) of getting the cancer. Mammary cancer can be fatal, and spaying is the one critical measure that you can take to prevent it.

Pyometra is a life-threatening infection of the uterus that can occur after a heat cycle. Pyometra generally occurs in middle-aged to older female dogs in the 6 weeks after heat. The hormone progesterone causes the blood-filled uterine lining to proliferate, and it also suppresses immune function in the uterus so that vaginal bacteria can ascend into the uterus and cause infection. With pyometra, the uterus swells extensively as it becomes filled with pus, bacteria, dying or dead tissue, and toxins. The treatment is to give antibiotics and spay immediately, otherwise the infection is nearly always fatal. Pyometra is quite common in older, unspayed females.

Unlike humans, dogs don't go into menopause, and a bitch will have heat cycles for her entire life, so these risks never go away. That's why spaying is one of the most important preventive measures that can be taken for a dog's health.

Males

Male dogs have both behavioral and medical benefits from being altered. The behavioral changes are those influenced by testosterone, which means interest in roaming is almost entirely eliminated—more than 60 percent of neutered dogs don't roam following sterilization.

Male dogs receive behavioral and medical benefits from being altered.

Aggressive behavior toward other male dogs also is reduced in 60 percent of neutered males. Urine marking is eliminated in 50 percent, and inappropriate mounting is eliminated in 70 percent. However, a male dog's playfulness and socialization with people is not altered at all (no pun intended).

Beneficial health consequences are significant, particularly concerning the prostate gland. Unless the testosterone level is reduced by neutering, the prostate gland usually enlarges gradually as a male dog ages. By the time he reaches senior status, the prostate is likely to have become uncomfortable. Some dogs have difficulty defecating because the enlarged prostate can displace the colon. Also, the likelihood of getting an infection of the prostate is lessened with neutering.

Social Concerns

The world has too many unwanted dogs who end up being euthanized because there simply aren't enough homes for all of them. Altering your pets is a socially conscious act. A stitch in time saves nine! Well, probably a lot more than nine, but you get the

idea. Unless you plan to become a responsible breeder and contribute to the overall improvement of the Miniature Schnauzer breed, alter your pets to prevent pet overpopulation—and unnecessary death.

ALTERNATIVE MEDICINE

The phrase *holistic medicine* emphasizes treatment of the whole body, including the dog's physical, mental, emotional, social, and spiritual concerns. Western or *allopathic medicine* is based on treating systems rather than the body as a whole.

The formal branches of alternative medicine include chiropractic, acupuncture, homeopathy, and herbal therapy. Many related fields also exist, such as Shiatsu, Reiki and dozens of other. Many people believe in these practices wholeheartedly; many others think they're bunk. Only you can decide if it's appropriate for your dog and your sensibilities.

You may find some terms in holistic medicine are just a bit too "New Age" for you. If you are uncomfortable with discussions of vital force and energy, focus on what can be accomplished rather than on the underlying concept. Allopathic medicine has limitations, and you may find that alternative medicine can help your Schnauzer in ways that traditional medicine cannot—and vice versa. When using alternative medicine, it is just as important to find a good practitioner as it is in allopathic medicine. Find one with training appropriate to the services being offered.

People who bring their pets to alternative practitioners generally have one of two reasons for doing so: They've had alternative treatment themselves and found it helpful, or they are searching for something that will help their dog if allopathic medicine is not achieving desired results.

Homeopathy

Homeopathy's main principle is called the Law of Similars, in which like cures like. It treats disease with tiny quantities of substances that trigger the body's ability to fight a specific disease on its own. In other words, a substance that can cause symptoms of disease at normal doses can stimulate the body to fight and eradicate those symptoms in tiny doses. This is the basis of human allergy shots: Being exposed to tiny doses of something to which you're allergic, like pollen, makes you less sensitive to it.

In homeopathic medicine, a patient's symptoms are a reflection of an imbalance in that patient's inner force, sometimes called vital force.

Acupuncture

What's old is new again—acupuncture began almost 4,000 years ago in China. In the West, it has recently become popular in human and veterinary medicine. In acupuncture, specific points in the body are stimulated to help relieve pain or inflammation or encourage healing. These specific points are treated by needling, massage, and heat to balance the body. Painlessly inserting thin needles creates a physiologic response that can improve medical problems and sometimes behavioral issues such as fearfulness or compulsive disorders.

Studies of how acupuncture works, conducted in an effort to explain it in allopathic terms, indicate that it causes the release of hormones such as cortisol, natural painkillers like endorphins, and other substances. It stimulates tissue response and increases tissue blood supply. However, traditional acupuncture deals with energy and balance, which are not allopathic concerns.

Most dogs receiving acupuncture are treated for chronic health problems such as pain, arthritis, gastrointestinal disease, respiratory problems, skin conditions, and kidney disease. It's no surprise that most canine acupuncture patients are senior dogs. Acupuncture is also suggested for dogs undergoing chemotherapy, to reduce nausea and pain.

Chiropractic

Chiropractic care can certainly be used for dogs. When a joint doesn't move correctly, the dog's movement is adversely affected, and chiropractics addresses the mechanical causes of disease without using drugs.

Your dog's spine has over 100 joints. Many health problems in dogs can be attributed to vertebral subluxations that can cause or contribute to constant pain, muscle spasms, and even organ problems. Chiropractors define *subluxation* as an alteration in a joint's alignment, movement, or function, even though the joint is still intact. A *fixation* is another common chiropractic term that means a joint is immobilized. Canine chiropractors seek to remove subluxations or fixations by gently adjusting the spine or affected

Armed with the knowledge of genetic diseases that Mini Schnauzers are prone to, you can be alert to their signs and symptoms to help your dog live a full life.

joints back into proper alignment.

In some states in the United States, your veterinarian must refer you to a chiropractor. Most animal chiropractors are not veterinarians; they are usually licensed chiropractors who have also been certified to work

with animals. Some veterinarians, however, have also been certified in chiropractic care.

Herbs

Herbal remedies use preparations made from the leaves, roots, bark, flowers, and seeds of plants to promote healing. Many prescription drugs are chemical derivatives of compounds isolated from herbs. Although herbal remedies work more slowly than do prescription drugs, they can be effective. Herbs can affect the body in many positive ways, but they should be used cautiously and with the advice of someone familiar with both their good and bad effects. Consult an herbalist. Do not determine dosages and types of herbs on your own. A lot of misconception surrounds the potential harmlessness of natural medicines. Some people think that because a substance is natural, it cannot hurt a dog. Poppycock! Hemlock and snake venom are natural, too. A dose based on weight can be the difference between life and death. If a herb is strong enough to be effective, it's strong enough to be a problem if given in incorrect doses.

Its also possible for combinations of herbs to work against each other—or against prescription medication—rather than work in tandem. Always tell your vet if you are administering herbal remedies to your dog.

Numerous books are available to help you understand the concepts of herbalism and choose a competent herbalist.

SENIOR MINIATURE SCHNAUZERS

There's something wonderful about loving a geriatric dog—this period is one of the best you will share together. Miniature Schnauzers are incredibly appealing during this phase. A certain level of vulnerability can be seen in many canine senior citizens. Most dogs are calm, past those wild antics of their prime that have become family lore, and they are content to simply be by your side. At a veteran's performance at a conformation dog show, this group brings a stronger emotional response than any other—usually, there isn't a dry eye around the ring.

Medical

As Miniature Schnauzers age, their bodies change. Your senior dog's mind may wander a bit, or he may not seem as sharp as he was when younger. Remember: Most medical and mental conditions can be improved through veterinary intervention. Health problems can crop up quickly in seniors, and these problems are easier to correct when diagnosed early, rather than after they've taken root. Vigilantly look for lumps, bumps, discharges, and warts. Keep an eye on bodily functions, such as hearing, seeing, eliminating, chewing, eating, walking, and getting up. Don't worry if he no longer wants to chase the cat, but bring him to the vet if he won't stop vomiting.

Take your Miniature Schnauzer to the vet for routine screening more often, usually twice a year instead of annually. Most senior dogs must visit the vet more often than before, so you may not need to schedule routine visits on top of those for medical need.

If your senior is scheduled for surgery, even just a dental, opt for the presurgical blood test. It can indicate several factors that may have a bearing on anesthesia and thus on the safety of the surgery.

First-Aid Kit

Having a first-aid kit for your dog is practical as well as comforting. You can buy a commercially prepared one, or you can create your own.

Each first-aid kit should include appropriate phone numbers, such as your regular clinic and your emergency hospital, as well as the Poison Control Center for Animals. Most of these supplies are available at pet supply stores and veterinary clinics.

Basic supplies include:

- Scissors to cut tape and gauze and to clip hair around wounds
- Triple antibiotic ointment to promote wound healing
- Iodine prep solution, an antiseptic solution for cleaning wounds
- Gauze pads
- Gauze rolls
- Alcohol pads to clean scissors and tweezers
- Vet wrap, a flexible bandage that sticks to itself without need of tape or clips
- Latex gloves for you to wear so you don't contaminate a wound
- Muzzle (gauze rolls can be fashioned into a temporary muzzle, because even the friendliest dog in the world may bite the person he most loves when in pain)
- Eye wash
- Antiseptic solution for cleansing wounds
- Tweezers
- First-aid information
- Three-percent hydrogen peroxide to induce vomiting in case of poisoning

Diet and Exercise

Keeping a dog's weight under control is important, because obesity increases the risk of or exacerbates many diseases. On the other hand, some older dogs show a decreased interest in their food, and new foods to are needed to stimulate appetite. A higher calorie food may be needed if the dog loses too much weight. Generally speaking, as some dogs age, they may need less protein because of decreasing kidney function. But some senior dogs may need as much protein as usual to help maintain muscle mass and function. Ask your vet to help you choose the food with the best protein levels for your older dog. The need for exercise typically lessens with age, but that doesn't mean your Schnauzer is willing to forego daily walks. Forget about that! The walk may be shorter, and on days of poor health, it can be skipped, but let your dog decide if a walk is on today's schedule.

Using a human first-aid kit is not in your dog's best interest, because some things for people should not used on pets, such as adhesive medical tape and ibuprofen. It's often convenient, however, to put both pet and human supplies into one first-aid kit. Some people keep one first-aid kit at home and one in the car.

One critical component of a first-aid kit is written information on what you should do for a specific type of injury. Buy a pet first-aid book, and keep it with the kit. All that stuff in the first-aid kit isn't going to help if you use it incorrectly. An owner who is inexperienced in first aid and panicked about her dog may not be able to figure out what to do in an emergency without a written guide, even with appropriate supplies. For example, if you wrap the vet wrap too tightly, you'll cut off the circulation. That's one of the benefits of buying a commercially prepared kit—that kind of information is usually included.

It's important to know how to transport an injured dog. While a Miniature Schnauzer is small enough to be carried, there might be times when carrying him is not the best idea. Have a towel or blanket in your car specifically for this purpose.

Comfort

Miniature Schnauzers never lose their need for grooming, but you may need to change how you go about it, aiming for comfort as the primary concern. Mats in the coat can cause irritation to the skin, and those still must be taken care of. Sometimes it is less stressful for your senior if you just cut a mat out rather than comb it out. Alter his grooming to suit his physical needs.

Thicker bedding may be needed to protect old bones from hard, cold floors, and an older dog may feel cold more easily than he used to. If necessary, provide orthopedic bedding or clothing. Heated orthopedic beds are available. Your Mini may follow you everywhere in the house, so having more beds available might help. Ramps or steps can assist your Mini in getting up on furniture or the bed independently.

THE AMERICAN KENNEL CLUB BREED STANDARD

General Appearance

The Miniature Schnauzer is a robust, active dog of terrier type, resembling his larger cousin, the Standard Schnauzer, in general appearance, and of an alert, active disposition. *Faults—Type—*Toyishness, ranginess or coarseness.

Size, Proportion, Substance

*Size—*From 12 to 14 inches. He is sturdily built, nearly square in *proportion* of body length to height with plenty of bone, and without any suggestion of toyishness. *Disqualifications—*Dogs or bitches under 12 inches or over 14 inches.

Head

*Eyes—*Small, dark brown and deep-set. They are oval in appearance and keen in *expression*. *Faults—*Eyes light and/or large and prominent in appearance. *Ears—*When cropped, the ears are identical in shape and length, with pointed tips. They are in balance with the head and not exaggerated in length. They are set high on the skull and carried perpendicularly at the inner edges, with as little bell as possible along the outer edges. When uncropped, the ears are small and V-shaped, folding close to the skull. *Head* strong and rectangular, its width diminishing slightly from ears to eyes, and again to the tip of the nose. The forehead is unwrinkled. The *topskull* is flat and fairly long. The foreface is parallel to the topskull, with a slight stop, and it is at least as long as the topskull. The *muzzle* is strong in proportion to the skull; it ends in a moderately blunt manner, with thick whiskers which accentuate the rectangular shape of the head. *Faults—*Head coarse and cheeky. The *teeth* meet in a *scissors bite*. That is, the upper front teeth overlap the lower front teeth in such a manner that the inner surface of the upper incisors barely touches the outer surface of the lower incisors when the mouth is closed. *Faults—*Bite—Undershot or overshot jaw. Level bite.

Neck, Topline, Body

*Neck—*strong and well arched, blending into the shoulders, and with the skin fitting tightly at the throat. *Body* short and deep, with the brisket extending at least to the elbows. Ribs are well sprung and deep, extending well back to a short loin. The underbody does not present a tucked up appearance at the flank. The *backline* is straight; it declines slightly from the withers to the base of the tail. The withers form the highest point of the body. The overall length from chest to buttocks appears to equal the height at the withers. *Faults—*Chest too broad or shallow in brisket. Hollow or roach back. *Tail* set high and carried erect. It is docked only long enough to be clearly visible over the backline of the body when the dog is in proper length of coat. *Fault—*Tail set too low.

Forequarters

Forelegs are straight and parallel when viewed from all sides. They have strong pasterns and good bone. They are separated by a fairly deep brisket which precludes a pinched front. The elbows are close, and the ribs spread gradually from the first rib so as to allow space for the elbows to move close to the body. *Fault—*Loose elbows. The sloping *shoulders* are muscled, yet flat and clean. They are well laid back, so that from the side the tips of the shoulder blades are in a nearly vertical line above the elbow. The tips of the blades are placed closely together. They slope forward and downward at an angulation which permits the maximum forward extension of the forelegs without binding or effort. Both the shoulder blades and upper arms are long, permitting depth of chest at the brisket. *Feet* short and round (cat feet) with thick, black pads. The toes are arched and compact.

Hindquarters

The hindquarters have strong-muscled, slanting thighs. They are well bent at the stifles. There is sufficient angulation so that, in stance, the hocks extend beyond the tail. The hindquarters never appear overbuilt or higher than the shoulders. The rear pasterns are short and, in stance, perpendicular to the ground and, when viewed from the rear, are parallel to each other. *Faults—*Sickle hocks, cow hocks, open hocks or bowed hindquarters.

Coat

Double, with hard, wiry, outer coat and close undercoat. The head, neck, ears, chest, tail, and body coat must be plucked. When in show condition, the body coat should be of sufficient length to determine texture. Close covering on neck, ears and skull. Furnishings are fairly thick but not silky. *Faults—*Coat too soft or too smooth and slick in appearance.

Color

The recognized colors are salt and pepper, black and silver and solid black. All colors have uniform skin pigmentation, i.e. no white or pink skin patches shall appear anywhere on the dog.

Salt and Pepper—The typical salt and pepper color of the topcoat results from the combination of black and white banded hairs and solid black and white unbanded hairs, with the banded hairs predominating. Acceptable are all shades of salt and pepper, from light to dark mixtures with tan shadings permissible in the banded or unbanded hair of the topcoat. In salt and pepper dogs, the salt and pepper mixture fades out to light gray or silver white in the eyebrows, whiskers, cheeks, under throat, inside ears, across chest, under tail, leg furnishings, and inside hind legs. It may or may not also fade out on the underbody. However, if so, the lighter underbody hair is not to rise higher on the sides of the body than the front elbows. ***Black and Silver***—The black and silver generally follows the same pattern as the salt and pepper. The entire salt and pepper section must be black. The black color in the topcoat of the black and silver is a true rich color with black undercoat. The stripped portion is free from any fading or brown tinge and the underbody should be dark. ***Black***—Black is the only solid color allowed. Ideally, the black color in the topcoat is a true rich glossy solid color with the undercoat being less intense, a soft matting shade of black. This is natural and should not be penalized in any way. The stripped portion is free from any fading or brown tinge. The scissored and clippered areas have lighter shades of black. A small white spot on the chest is permitted, as is an occasional single white hair elsewhere on the body. ***Disqualifications***—Color solid white or white striping, patching, or spotting on the colored areas of the dog, except for the small white spot permitted on the chest of the black. The body coat color in salt and pepper and black and silver dogs fades out to light gray or silver white under the throat and across the chest. Between them there exists a natural body coat color. Any irregular or connecting blaze or white mark in this section is considered a white patch on the body, which is also a disqualification. .

Gait
The trot is the gait at which movement is judged. When approaching, the forelegs, with elbows close to the body, move straight forward, neither too close nor too far apart. Going away, the hind legs are straight and travel in the same planes as the forelegs. *Note—It is generally accepted that when a full trot is achieved, the rear legs continue to move in the same planes as the forelegs, but a very slight inward inclination will occur. It begins at the point of the shoulder in front and at the hip joint in the rear. Viewed from the front or rear, the legs are straight from these points to the pads. The degree of inward inclination is almost imperceptible in a Miniature Schnauzer that has correct movement. It does not justify moving close, toeing in, crossing, or moving out at the elbows.* Viewed from the side, the forelegs have good reach, while the hind legs have strong drive, with good pickup of hocks. The feet turn neither inward nor outward. ***Faults***—Single tracking, sidegaiting, paddling in front, or hackney action. Weak rear action.

Temperament
The typical Miniature Schnauzer is alert and spirited, yet obedient to command. He is friendly, intelligent and willing to please. He should never be overaggressive or timid.

Disqualifications
Dogs or bitches under 12 inches or over 14 inches.
Color solid white or white striping, patching, or spotting on the colored areas of the dog, except for the small white spot permitted on the chest of the black. The body coat color in salt and pepper and black and silver dogs fades out to light gray or silver white under the throat and across the chest. Between them there exists a natural body coat color. Any irregular or connecting blaze or white mark in this section is considered a white patch on the body, which is also a disqualification.
Approved January 15, 1991
Effective February 27, 1991

THE KENNEL CLUB BREED STANDARD

General Appearance
Sturdily built, robust, sinewy, nearly square, (length of body equal to height at shoulders). Expression keen and attitude alert. Correct conformation is of more importance than colour or other purely 'beauty' points.

Characteristics
Well balanced, smart, stylish and adaptable.

Temperament
Alert, reliable and intelligent. Primarily a companion dog.

Head and Skull
Head strong and of good length, narrowing from ears to eyes and then gradually forward toward

end of nose. Upper part of the head (occiput to the base of forehead) moderately broad between ears. Flat, creaseless forehead; well muscled but not too strongly developed cheeks. Medium stop to accentuate prominent eyebrows. Powerful muzzle ending in a moderately blunt line, with bristly, stubby moustache and chin whiskers. Ridge of nose straight and running almost parallel to extension of forehead. Nose black with wide nostrils. Lips tight but not overlapping.

Eyes
Medium-sized, dark, oval, set forward, with arched bushy eyebrows.

Ears
Neat, V-shaped, set high and dropping forward to temple.

Mouth
Jaws strong with perfect, regular and complete scissor bite, i.e. upper teeth closely overlapping lower teeth and set square to the jaws.

Neck
Moderately long, strong and slightly arched; skin close to throat; neck set cleanly on shoulders.

Forequarters
Shoulders flat and well laid. Forelegs straight viewed from any angle. Muscles smooth and lithe rather than prominent; bone strong, straight and carried well down to feet; elbows close to body and pointing directly backwards.

Body
Chest moderately broad, deep with visible strong breastbone reaching at least to height of elbow rising slightly backward to loins. Back strong and straight, slightly higher at shoulder than at hindquarters, with short, well developed loins. Ribs well sprung. Length of body equal to height from top of withers to ground.

Hindquarters
Thighs slanting and flat but strongly muscled. Hindlegs (upper and lower thighs) at first vertical to the stifle; from stifle to hock, in line with the extension of the upper neck line; from hock, vertical to ground.

Feet
Short, round, cat-like, compact with closely arched toes, dark nails, firm black pads, feet pointing forward.

Tail
Customarily docked. Docked: Set on and carried high, customarily docked to three joints. Undocked: Set on and carried high, of moderate length to give general balance to the dog. Thick at root and tapering towards the tip, as straight as possible, carried jauntily

Gait/Movement
Free, balanced and vigorous, with good reach in forequarters and good driving power in hindquarters. Topline remains level in action.

Coat
Harsh, wiry and short enough for smartness, dense undercoat. Clean on neck and shoulders, ears and skull. Harsh hair on legs. Furnishings fairly thick but not silky.

Colour
All pepper and salt colours in even proportions, or pure black, or black and silver. That is, solid black with silver markings on eyebrow, muzzle, chest and brisket and on the forelegs below the point of elbow, on inside of hindlegs below the stifle joint, on vent and under tail.

Size
Ideal height: dogs: 36 cms (14 ins); bitches: 33 cms (13 ins). Too small, toyish appearing dogs are not typical and undesirable.

Faults
Any departure from the foregoing points should be considered a fault and the seriousness with which the fault should be regarded should be in exact proportion to its degree and its effect upon the health and welfare of the dog.

Note
Male animals should have two apparently normal testicles fully descended into the scrotum.
July 2001

ASSOCIATIONS AND ORGANIZATIONS

BREED CLUBS

American Kennel Club (AKC)
5580 Centerview Drive
Raleigh, NC 27606
Telephone: (919) 233-9767
Fax: (919) 233-3627
E-mail: info@akc.org
www.akc.org

Canadian Kennel Club (CKC)
89 Skyway Avenue, Suite 100
Etobicoke, Ontario M9W 6R4
Telephone: (416) 675-5511
Fax: (416) 675-6506
E-mail: information@ckc.ca
www.ckc.ca

The American Miniature
Schnauzer Club (AMSC)
Secretary: Terrie Houck
E-mail: secretary@amsc.us
www.amsc.us

The Kennel Club
1 Clarges Street
London
W1J 8AB
Telephone: 0870 606 6750
Fax: 0207 518 1058
www.the-kennel-club.org.uk

The Schnauzer Club of Great Britain (SCGB)
www.schnauzerclub.co.uk/

United Kennel Club (UKC)
100 E. Kilgore Road
Kalamazoo, MI 49002-5584
Telephone: (269) 343-9020
Fax: (269) 343-7037
E-mail: pbickell@ukcdogs.com
www.ukcdogs.com

RESCUE ORGANIZATIONS AND ANIMAL WELFARE GROUPS

American Humane Association (AHA)
63 Inverness Drive East
Englewood, CO 80112
Telephone: (303) 792-9900
Fax: 792-5333
www.americanhumane.org

American Society for the Prevention of Cruelty to Animals (ASPCA)
424 E. 92nd Street
New York, NY 10128-6804
Telephone: (212) 876-7700
www.aspca.org

Royal Society for the Prevention of Cruelty to Animals (RSPCA)
Telephone: 0870 3335 999
Fax: 0870 7530 284
www.rspca.org.uk

The Humane Society of the United States (HSUS)
2100 L Street, NW
Washington DC 20037
Telephone: (202) 452-1100
www.hsus.org

SPORTS

Canine Freestyle Federation, Inc.
Membership Secretary: Brandy Clymire
E-mail: CFFmemberinfo@aol.com
www.canine-freestyle.org

International Agility Link (IAL)
Global Administrator: Steve Drinkwater
E-mail: yunde@powerup.au
www.agilityclick.com/~ial

North American Flyball Association (NAFA)
1400 West Devon Avenue #512
Chicago, IL 60660
Telephone: (800) 318-6312
Fax: (800) 318-6318
www.flyball.org

VETERINARY RESOURCES

Academy of Veterinary Homeopathy (AVH)
P.O. Box 9280
Wilmington, DE 19809
Telephone: (866) 652-1590
Fax: (866) 652-1590
E-mail: office@TheAVH.org
www.theavh.org

American Academy of Veterinary Acupuncture (AAVA)
100 Roscommon Drive, Suite 320
Middletown, CT 06457
Telephone: (860) 635-6300
Fax: (860) 635-6400
E-mail: office@aava.org
www.aava.org

American Animal Hospital Association (AAHA)
P.O. Box 150899
Denver, CO 80215-0899
Telephone: (303) 986-2800
Fax: (303) 986-1700
E-mail: info@aahanet.org
www.aahanet.org/index.cfm

American Holistic Veterinary Medical Association (AHVMA)
2218 Old Emmorton Road
Bel Air, MD 21015
Telephone: (410) 569-0795
Fax: (410) 569-2346
E-mail: office@ahvma.org
www.ahvma.org

American Veterinary Medical Association (AVMA)
1931 North Meacham Road – Suite 100
Schaumburg, IL 60173
Telephone: (847) 925-8070
Fax: (847) 925-1329
E-mail: avmainfo@avma.org
www.avma.org

British Veterinary Association (BVA)
7 Mansfield Street
London
W1G 9NQ
Telephone: 020 7636 6541
Fax: 020 7436 2970
E-mail: bvahq@bva.co.uk
www.bva.co.uk

MISCELLANEOUS

Association of Pet Dog Trainers (APDT)
150 Executive Center Drive
Box 35
Greenville, SC 29615
Telephone: (800) PET-DOGS
Fax: (864) 331-0767
E-mail: information@apdt.com
www.apdt.com

Delta Society
875 124th Ave NE, Suite 101
Bellevue, WA 98005
Telephone: (425) 226-7357
Fax: (425) 235-1076
E-mail: info@deltasociety.org
www.deltasociety.org

Therapy Dogs International (TDI)
88 Bartley Road
Flanders, NJ 07836
Telephone: (973) 252-9800
Fax: (973) 252-7171
E-mail: tdi@gti.net
www.tdi-dog.org

PUBLICATIONS

BOOKS

Lane, Dick, and Neil Ewart. *A-Z of Dog Diseases & Health Problems*. New York: Howell Books, 1997.

Rubenstein, Eliza, and Shari Kalina. *The Adoption Option: Choosing and Raising the Shelter Dog for You*. New York: Howell Books, 1996.

Serpell, James. *The Domestic Dog: Its Evolution, Behaviour and Interactions with People*. Cambridge: Cambridge University Press, 1995.

MAGAZINES

AKC Family Dog
American Kennel Club
260 Madison Avenue
New York, NY 10016
Telephone: (800) 490-5675
E-mail: familydog@akc.org
www.akc.org/pubs/familydog

AKC Gazette
American Kennel Club
260 Madison Avenue
New York, NY 10016
Telephone: (800) 533-7323
E-mail: gazette@akc.org
www.akc.org/pubs/gazette

Dog & Kennel
Pet Publishing, Inc.
7-L Dundas Circle
Greensboro, NC 27407
Telephone: (336) 292-4272
Fax: (336) 292-4272
E-mail: info@petpublishing.com
www.dogandkennel.com

Dog Fancy
Subscription Department
P.O. Box 53264
Boulder, CO 80322-3264
Telephone: (800) 365-4421
E-mail: barkback@dogfancy.com
www.dogfancy.com

Dogs Monthly
Ascot House
High Street, Ascot,
Berkshire SL5 7JG
United Kingdom
Telephone: 0870 730 8433
Fax: 0870 730 8431
E-mail: admin@rtc-associates.freeserve.co.uk
www.corsini.co.uk/dogsmonthly

WEBSITES

Dog-Play
www.dog-play.com/ethics.html
A cornucopia of information and pertinent links on responsible dog breeding.

The Dog Speaks
www.thedogspeaks.com
Canine Behaviorist Deb Duncan's site, filled with useful advice on canine etiquette, behavior problems, communication, and relevant links.

Petfinder
www.petfinder.org
Search shelters and rescue groups for adoptable pets.

ACKNOWLEDGEMENTS

I'd like to thank the following people for all of their help, some of whom kindly shared a significant amount of their time and expertise: Linda Sullivan, DVM; Karen Brittan of Britmor Schnauzers; Pat and Jim Discher of PJ's Doghouse; Debra Eldredge, DVM; Elizabeth Lundgren, DVM; Anne Kelly; Chris Larson; Peg Banks; Becky Alder; Bernd Guenter; Darlene Arden; Chris Walkowicz; and Gina Spadafori.

ABOUT THE AUTHOR

Phyllis DeGioia is an award-winning writer who specializes in writing about dogs, particularly health issues. A member of the Dog Writers Association of America, she has been published in numerous pet publications and has blogged for *The Bark* magazine. As editor of www.veterinarypartner.com, she regularly works with veterinarians and pet experts on informative articles for pet owners. She lives in Madison, Wisconsin, with three dogs and a scaredy cat, all of whom are rescues.

PHOTO CREDITS

Photos on pages 22, 60, 64, 82, 109, 128, 133, 135, 148, and 176 courtesy of Paulette Braun.
Photos on pages 75, 140, and 144 courtesy of Robert Pearcy.
Photos on pages 24, 79, 114, 155, and 185 courtesy of Vince Serbin.
Photos on pages 115 and 136 courtesy of Pet Profiles by Lara Stern.
Author photo courtesy of Daniel Olson.
All other photos courtesy of Isabelle Francais and T.F.H. archives.